GENDER IMAGES
in PUBLIC ADMINISTRATION

Second Edition

GENDER IMAGES in PUBLIC ADMINISTRATION

Second Edition

Legitimacy
and the
Administrative
State

Camilla Stivers

Maxine Goodman Levin College of Urban Affairs
Cleveland State University, Ohio

SAGE Publications
International Educational and Professional Publisher
Thousand Oaks ▪ London ▪ New Delhi

For information:

Sage Publications, Inc.
2455 Teller Road
Thousand Oaks, California 91320
E-mail: order@sagepub.com

Sage Publications Ltd.
6 Bonhill Street
London EC2A 4PU
United Kingdom

Sage Publications India Pvt. Ltd.
M-32 Market
Greater Kailash I
New Delhi 110 048 India

Library of Congress Cataloging-in-Publication Data

Stivers, Camilla.
  Gender images in public administration Legitimacy
and the administrative state / by Camilla Stivers.--2nd ed.
     p. cm.
   ISBN 0-7619-2173-7 (c) -- ISBN 0-7619-2174-5 (p)
   1. Women in public life--United States. 2. Women in the civil
service--United States. 3. Sex role--United States. 4. Public
administration--United States. I. Title.
   HQ1391.U5 S75 2002
   305.42´0973--dc21

                                        2002001786

02   03   04   05   06   07   10   9   8   7   6   5   4   3   2   1

Acquisitions Editor	:	Marquita Flemming
Editorial Assistant	:	MaryAnn Vail
Production Editor	:	Diana E. Axelsen
Copy Editor	:	Joyce Kuhn
Typesetter	:	Siva Math Setters, Chennai, India
Indexer	:	Jeanne Busemeyer
Cover Designer	:	Sandra Ng

Contents

Preface

Quite often, when I talk to classes of public administration students about gender, someone—woman or man—says, "Well, I'm sure it was like that in the bad old days, but things have changed." More than any other single factor, this comment (heard over and over) led me to produce a second edition of *Gender Images*. The first edition was written in 1991 and came out in print in late 1992, so it has been nearly a decade since I did the supporting research. Perhaps, I thought, things *had* changed; at least I owed it to the students, and to other readers of the book, to find out. The result is this new edition, which incorporates data, research studies, and theoretical literature from the past 10 years.

Unhappily, although there are signs of progress in such indicators as the proportions of women at upper levels of federal, state, and local governments, in my judgment the big picture as seen in the field's writings looks pretty much the way it did 10 years ago. Public administration scholarship continues to rely on images that conform to widely accepted (though varied) notions of masculinity, and women are still struggling to manage their gender images (not too feminine, not too masculine) and to balance competing demands of work and family. And even more unhappily, with a few exceptions, by and large the literature in the field still neglects the issue of gender. If for no other reason, since it is common for a majority of the students in an MPA class to be women, we still seem to need a book that considers gender as a factor in public administration—and of course, there are lots of other reasons, as this book tries to show.

A few readers of the first edition responded to it by calling *Gender Images* a "polemic." (A roughly equal number told me I was too timid.) My dictionary defines a polemic as "a controversy or argument, esp. one that is a refutation of or an attack upon a specified opinion or doctrine," so I suppose in the main these critics are right, since my intent is certainly to make an argument and to stimulate controversy. The purpose of my project has never been to attack in an intemperate way, however, but rather to engage in a dialogue. I do accept what my experience tells me, that raising the issue of gender (let alone the topic of feminist theory) is liable to be viewed as an act of aggression in some quarters.

Some have characterized the work of a number of feminist critics of organizations, including mine, as arbitrary and biased—that is, that we "read in masculinities whenever [we] feel like it," ignore the factors that promote equality between the sexes, and in general "oversensitize" the issue of gender (Alvesson & Billing, 1997, pp. 7, 12, 86). Readers of this new edition must judge for themselves whether this is the case. It seems to me that broaching the subject of gender in a field where it has been virtually absent can only be seen as oversensitivity by those who would rather the topic not be discussed at all. I have tried to make my argument judiciously and in a spirit of self-criticism. Gender analysis is neither self-evident nor the most important framework within which to approach the study of public administration. I do insist that a feminist perspective on gender in organizations makes it possible to see certain aspects that other perspectives do not reveal. The significance of the feminist perspective in comparison with others, I leave for readers to decide for themselves.

Reaching the finish line of this edition, like the previous one, was made possible only with the help and support of many colleagues and friends. My husband, Ralph Hummel, not only makes my world but sometimes finds himself offering feminist perspectives. He is my best critic and best friend. Colleagues and students at Cleveland State University, the University of Akron, and the Evergreen State College took on the earlier edition in lively discussions, as did classes at a number of universities where I was lucky enough to have the opportunity to talk. Many scholars in the field have helped me sharpen and refine my arguments, whether they considered themselves fellow travelers or unbelievers. My thanks to (in no particular order) Mary Ellen Guy, David Farmer, Suzanne Mettler, Chuck Fox and Hugh Miller, Jay White, Celia Davies, David Carnevale, Mary Timney, Cynthia McSwain and Orion White, Ken Dolbeare, Cheryl Simrell King, Matthew Holden, Dolores Foley, David Rosenbloom, Jennifer Alexander, Guy Adams, Richard Box, April Hejka-Ekins, Larry Terry, Cindy Rosenthal, Dick Pratt, J. J. Hendricks, Joyce Outshoorn, Petra Schreurs, and an anonymous reviewer. Conversations at the 1994 conference on women and public policy, cosponsored by Erasmus University, Rotterdam, and the University of Leiden, were extraordinarily stimulating and helpful. A special thanks to Renee Nank, colleague and friend, whose help and support anchor and guide me in so many ways. Ruth-Ellen Joeres continues to be my home away from home. The book is better for the criticism and appreciation it has received; its deficiencies remain my responsibility.

1

Gender and Public Administration

Skepticism about bureaucrats is an ongoing American phenomenon; the late 20th century, however, seemed to reach something of a nadir in the fortunes of public administration. Civil servants bore the brunt of widespread public suspicion and outright disapproval. Trading on the reported failure of the War on Poverty, budget deficits, and a series of scandals that sharpened American misgivings about government activism, politicians promised to lower taxes and reduce the size of the bureaucracy. Then-President Bill Clinton assured Americans that the era of big government was over. Seen by the public as paper shufflers and time servers, enmeshed in red tape and out of touch with reality, federal bureaucrats eagerly embraced the National Performance Review, and their counterparts at the state and local level took up their own efforts to "reinvent government" (Osborne & Gaebler, 1992).

Not surprisingly, the onslaught of criticism produced not just steps toward reform inside the bureaucracy but also a wave of efforts on the part of scholars to defend the work bureaucrats do, to justify the place that career administrators hold in the American system of government. In a representative system of government, legitimate power is seen as flowing from the people to their elected representatives and indirectly to appointed officials. The power of those who govern is checked by the fact that citizens can vote them out of office or at least vote out those who appointed them. In such a system, the exercise of power by civil servants, neither elected nor easily removable, is problematic.

A hundred years or so ago, when government—especially the federal government—was small and weak, when there was no "administrative state" to speak of, and when government jobs could be won through party loyalty, there was little need to defend the legitimacy of administrative power. But with increased responsibility and authority came increased need to counter accusations that the bureaucracy oppresses rather than serves American citizens. The need produced an outpouring of books, special journal issues, and conference presentations aimed at validating public administration.

Many of these defenses have drawn attention to qualities of the public service that are thought to be essential to good government and have summoned up corresponding images of public administrators as professional experts, good managers, and creative leaders. The thrust of these justifications is that the scale and complexity of contemporary society demand a stable class of career officials who can be counted on to have the competence, the vision, and the public spirit to steer the ship of state (Mitchell & Scott, 1987).

During the same period that public administration labored to defend itself, an equal or greater volume of writing called into question the gender dimensions of several centuries of Western political philosophy. Feminist theorizing critiqued the classical liberal state for its marked individualism and for the dependence of its clear boundary between public and private spheres on the exclusion of women and women's concerns from political life. Feminist theory offered new ideas about power, about the nature of organizations, and about leadership and professionalism; it brought to light fundamental ways in which women have shaped society and politics. Yet few of these ideas have made their way into conversations in public administration, and defenses of the administrative state still show little apparent consciousness that the images of public administration on which they rely have gender dimensions or that feminist political theory might have a significant role to play in the legitimacy project.

One could argue that apologists for the administrative state seem insensitive to gender because an enterprise so roundly criticized by politicians and the public at large hardly needs another source of critique. What help to public administration could a feminist point of view possibly be? Probably little, it would appear, if (as many of the current defenses suggest) justifying public administration involves simply mobilizing support for administrative business as usual. My assumption is, however, that public administration's legitimacy crisis (if crisis it is) has deeper roots than the failure of the War on Poverty, Watergate, Iran-Contra, Whitewater, or the Lewinsky scandal. If this is so, the need to defend public administration cannot be answered by an argument that restricts itself to currently accepted alternatives.

The thesis of this book is that images of professional expertise, management, leadership, and public virtue that mark justifications of administrative power contain dilemmas of gender. They not only have features commonly and unthinkingly associated with masculinity but they also help to keep in place or bestow political and economic privilege on the bearers of masculine qualities at the expense of those who display culturally feminine ones. Far from being superficial window-dressing or a side effect, the characteristic masculinity of public administration—though far from monolithic—is systemic: It contributes to and is sustained by power relations in society at large that distribute resources on the basis of gender (though not solely on this basis) and affect people's life chances and their sense of themselves and their place in the world.

Looking at public administration through the lens of gender, its public dimensions are revealed as gendered rather than neutral. Public administration involves the discretionary exercise of public power, and we expect public power to justify itself. Typically, this is accomplished by reference to redeeming features such as the public interest dimensions of administrative decision making, the expertise that is said to serve the public good, the deft management skills that make possible the accomplishment of public purposes, and the necessity for administrative leadership in an era of postindustrial complexity. But this publicness is problematic, because it is grounded in a historical understanding of the public sphere as a male preserve, distinct from the domestic realm that has been the primary life space and responsibility of women.

Classical liberalism has always seen boundaries around the public sphere as necessary to prevent tyranny by sheltering individual "private" concerns from the reach of the state. But paradoxically, the viability of the economic and political activities that go on in the liberal public sphere depends on the household: on the provision of shelter, food, clothing, and the bearing and nurturing of children. Both pervasively in theory and persistently in practice, the household has been viewed as the realm of women. Women's concerns, when they revolve around their domestic responsibilities, have been seen as private by definition—that is, as not political, not of public interest. Therefore, not only the justice of household arrangements but also *the division of human concerns into public and private* in the first place are barred from public discussion. (During a conference roundtable discussion, I once heard a male colleague ask, in reference to domestic violence, "When did this get defined as a public issue?" A female colleague replied, "When did it get defined as *not* a public issue?") Throughout history, women have been expected to handle needs related to sustenance and nurturance in order that men could have the time and energy for public pursuits (Jaggar, 1983; O'Brien, 1989; Okin, 1989). This division of labor persists today despite equal opportunity and affirmative action policies, which have simply enabled women to shoulder both household and paid work rather than to share them equally with men, and despite recommendations for shared parenting, which are honored more in the breach than in the observance (Hochschild, 1989; Rhode, 1988). In recent years, several theorists have suggested that the nature of the boundary between the public and private spheres is itself debatable—that is, it is a political issue (e.g., Ackelsberg & Shanley, 1996; Honig, 1993). If so, the justice of household arrangements can become a matter of public deliberation.

Like other public sector activities, public administration is structurally masculine despite its apparent neutrality and despite the presence of increasing numbers of women in federal, state, and local governments. It can only go on as it does with "business as usual" because women bear a lopsided share of the burden of domestic functions without which life would simply not be possible. Thus, justifications of public administration take place in a space that (a) depends for its coherence on the subordination of women through their assignment to a set of duties that, no matter how necessary, are generally regarded as less significant and (b) limits both women's opportunities to participate in public life and the time and energy they have to devote to it. (See Chapter 2 for extensive recent data on the division of household responsibilities, indicating that despite progress in the past decade, the structural problem I describe is still with us.)

The gender dimensions of this arrangement are paradoxical. The state depends on the household but acknowledges only grudgingly the political relevance of domestic issues; throughout liberal theory women are treated as "citizens," but in reality their participation in public life has been restricted, either formally (in law) or practically, by the demands of their household duties. It is this sort of gender paradox, which I argue constitutes a dilemma for women in the administrative state, that the book considers.

Examining gender dilemmas involves taking into account everyday life practices, such as what goes on in families, organizations, and politics, as well as what theorists say. It entails an effort to undo the taken-for-grantedness of administrative practices and what is written and thought about them: to bring to light ambiguities, gaps, contradictions, and unspoken assumptions that are connected to our varied notions of what constitutes appropriate masculine and feminine behavior—that is, gender. The intent is to articulate the harm these administrative ideas and patterns of behavior work on women and to lay the groundwork for the transformation of the thoughts and practices in question. I want to show that these widely accepted understandings (a) devalue a range of contributions and concerns that are thought to be associated with femininity and (b) limit women's political and social freedom. Gender dynamics do, of course, restrict men's options as well, because the scope of pursuits and behavioral styles they feel free to adopt is narrower than it would be if men did not have to worry about being thought "feminine." But in most cases, being a man remains an advantage in the acquisition of economic, political, and organizational power. If this were not the case, there would be relatively little need to call gender dynamics into question. Uncomfortable as it may be for many men and not a few women to encounter the idea that, despite progress, gender stereotypes still harm women more than men, that is the position taken in this book and supported by empirical evidence both here and in a plethora of other studies.

Examining gender dilemmas in public administration does not imply the view that other factors such as race and class are less important. Gender is tied to race and class; gender's importance is not as the sole source of domination but as a lens that enables one to see things that other lenses miss. In what follows, I try to be consistent about pointing to the interrelationships among the three factors—to show, for example, where the harmful effect of gender stereotypes is exacerbated by influences of race and class. I also try not to generalize about gender in ways that obscure the visibility of these influences (for example, I try not to take it for granted that problems faced by women of color or women who hold clerical positions are the same as those of professional white women).

My approach to gender dilemmas in public administration is to focus on images of professional expertise, leadership and management, and virtue that have characterized defenses of administrative power. I do not pretend to take on public administration as a whole (whatever the reader's own definition of that enterprise may be), although I think it needs taking on. In the main, the book is a consideration of what role certain ideas play in an important arena of public administration theorizing. It is an exercise in the political philosophy of public administration, in the sense that Dwight Waldo's (1948) *The Administrative State* described: a consideration of the nature of power and the public good in administrative contexts. Questions such as these can be discussed and debated, and arguments for and against particular positions can be supported by empirical evidence, but they cannot be answered once and for all. They are what William Connolly (1993) has called essentially contested questions—and, in fact, that is what makes them "political." Thus I am not out to *prove* but rather to *argue* that there are gender dilemmas in public administration. I hope to persuade rather than to convince.

Because of the connection I see between what we think and material realities in the world, I begin by considering through the lens of gender some things that are actually going on in the world of contemporary public administrative practice. Chapter 2 looks at the extent of women's historical progress as public employees, their current status in federal, state, and local governments, the peculiar nature of the organizational reality they experience, and the extent to which women's place in society at large is shaped by the administrative state. I examine the implications of these factors for our understanding of the nature of public organizational dynamics and of the special role in governance that public servants play. I suggest that facts such as that women are still paid less than men, generally do most of the lower-level work, are still not represented proportionately in the top levels of the bureaucracy, have trouble fitting into accepted managerial roles, experience sexual harassment in organizations, and work a double shift of home and job responsibilities are as tangible as many other factors in the real world of public administration to which observers have given considerably more attention. I argue that our commonsense notions of the administrative state are deeply dependent on traditions that privilege men and the pursuits considered typical of them over women and their work. Documenting these factors is necessary in order that my subsequent arguments have weight: If stereotypes about gender that inhabit ideas of leadership and expertise had no effect on the actual dynamics of administrative life and action, they would be considerably less troubling than they are.

The book then turns to three images in defense of public administration that I argue present women with dilemmas of gender; that is, these images set up expectations and impose implicit performance standards that are culturally masculine and that therefore women have greater difficulty meeting than do men. By asserting that prevalent normative images in public administration are "masculine," I do not mean to imply that masculinity is a monolithic construct; clearly it is not, as will become evident in the following pages. There is not one image of masculinity in public administration, there are several. Chapter 3 deals with the image of expertise found in the argument that public administration is a legitimate part of government because public administrators are expert professionals. The need for expertise is a central tenet of modern public administration and has been so at least since Woodrow Wilson (1887) put forward the idea that the duty of administrators was to carry out legislative mandates by means of scientific expertise, not to take sides on political questions. Administration was legitimate because it was neutral and objective. As the practice of expertise became increasingly professionalized over the past century, the idea that career administrators are in some sense "professionals" became widespread. Yet the question remains, as Federick C. Mosher's (1968) classic study put it, "How can a [professional] public service . . . be made to operate in a manner compatible with democracy?" (p. 3). In the course of trying to answer this question, writers in the field have tried to show that administration requires professional expertise; they have painted a portrait of the legitimate administrator as a professional expert. This image is marked by four dimensions my argument attempts to deconstruct: objectivity, autonomy, hierarchy, and brotherhood. I suggest that the image of expertise is fundamentally inconsistent with widely held notions of womanhood and the actual conditions of most women's lives, and I attempt to show the gender contradictions that lurk inside any attempt to join professional expertise with ideas of the public interest.

Chapter 4 considers the leadership of the public administrator and the argument that, in a system of government marked by separation of powers and interest group politics, someone has to steer the ship of state, to be the balance wheel or fulcrum in a fractionated system, to hold things together, to move them forward—to have a vision. I argue that this way of thinking about leadership works to keep in place dynamics of discrimination against women. Four images of public sector leadership are examined: the visionary, the decision maker, the symbol, and the definer of reality. As constituted, these ideals conflict with widely held expectations about women's behavior, requiring women to struggle with the tension between being feminine and being a leader, a tension that requires a continuing balancing act. I suggest that current images of leadership are at best an equivocal basis on which to defend administrative power.

Chapter 4 also examines the idea of the public administrator as a "manager," an increasingly popular idea connected with efforts to make public administration more businesslike and systematic. Woodrow Wilson (1887) said that "the field of administration is a field of business" (p. 209), a proposition that shaped the early days of the field but has taken on new resonance as "reinventing government," performance measurement, customer service, and the devolution of public responsibilities to the private sector have proliferated. The management perspective has taken a somewhat different tack from other legitimating strategies, for it has essentially adopted the position of the critics of bureaucracy instead of attempting to deflect it. In the management view, the critics are right, and the answer is to "break through bureaucracy," turn bureaucrats into innovators and entrepreneurs, and get rid of "bureau-pathology"—in sum, to make government agencies run like well-run businesses. Here, too, there are gender dilemmas, since the idea of "management" is rooted in historically and culturally masculine images.

In Chapter 5, I deal with arguments grounded in the public administrator's virtue or public spirit, such as those that suggest that public administrators are guardians or trustees of the public interest, or "heroes," or "exemplars of virtue," or "citizens for the rest of us." I suggest that images of virtue in American political history are fundamentally gendered and linked to a sex-based division of social life into public and domestic spheres that disadvantages women and hinders public administration from promoting a politically compelling version of virtue.

In Chapter 6, I examine the reform era out of which public administration as a field of study developed and in which so many of its ideas and arguments have their origins. The discussion aims to show how women's work and thought were at the center of the movement to reform city governments and how gender dynamics at the time resulted in a bifurcation between what could have been complementary impulses of systematization and caring. The extent to which the contemporary administrative state has roots in women's reform work has been obscured because male reformers, painted by party politicians as effeminate, felt the need to make public administration masculine by making it "muscular"—that is, scientific and businesslike.

In the final chapter, I reflect on some of the implications of the book's arguments—what gender dilemmas inherent in current defenses of public administration tell us about the direction in which it must head if the administrative state is to be a realm equally hospitable to women and men and fully equipped to operate effectively in the future without reliance on discriminatory ideas. My argument here is based on the notion that change depends not on introducing a missing element but on bringing to light factors that already inhabit our most taken-for-granted ideas and processes. In other words, gender is already present in public administration. How can we turn recognition of this fact and an analysis on this basis into transformative energy? I present several examples of how feminist thinking might work toward transformation.

Readers will have already noticed that this book is a "feminist" discussion. Feminism has apparently acquired something of a bad name over the past couple of decades. In countless conversations with women in public administration both before and after the first edition of this book was published, I encountered over and over the following paradox: Although most women in public service firmly support equal pay for equal work, equal access to jobs (including those at the top), the sharing of housework, and better child-care facilities, and many are interested in promoting what they see to be "feminine" qualities in the workplace, they are very likely to distance themselves from the term "feminism," which they equate either with academic abstraction or with shrill narrow-mindedness and even man hating. When I once asked during a conference panel discussion whether the ideas of Mary Parker Follett (public administration's one "grand old woman"; see Follett, 1918, 1924) might today be considered feminist, several women made it clear that they saw feminist as a derogatory term, one Follett "didn't deserve"—although one of the women I spoke to afterward admitted that as far as she knew she had never read a feminist book.

I have concluded from these many conversations that at the very least there is a risk associated in the minds of many professional women (and men) with counting themselves as feminists, one they would just as soon avoid. If so, I take a different risk by using the term—that is, of alienating women and men for whom it calls up a negative image. Since I hope to reach beyond the walls of academia to connect with women and men in public service, then, it seems especially important to be clear about what I mean when I use the term.

The first thing to say is that most feminist theorists today no longer believe that it is possible or even desirable to settle on one definition of feminism. Many writers now speak of "feminisms" as a way of acknowledging and even celebrating the diversity of viewpoints among women and men who want to take the impact of gender dynamics into account in developing a systematic understanding of how society works. Women of color have been a major force in moving feminist theory toward this position, but the tendency has been reinforced by the widespread realization that to universalize one version as "the" feminist worldview would be to replicate the fallacy of overgeneralization historically prevalent among male thinkers, in which observation and reasoning based in elite white men's experiences and concerns are applied equally to women, people of color, working class and poor people, and so on.

What, then, does the term feminism mean today? To what does it commit the person who speaks as a "feminist?" Three things, in my view: to the proposition that gender is a crucially useful category of analysis, to a critical perspective on women's current status and prospects, and, to use Gerda Lerner's words, to "a system of ideas and practices which assumes that men and women must share equally in the work, in the privileges, in the defining and the dreaming of the world" (quoted in Astin & Leland, 1991, p. 19).

With those propositions in mind, the most fundamental way to characterize a feminist approach is to say that the gender lens encourages one to see underlying assumptions (experiential and otherwise) that shape the concepts and conclusions that people display in their practices—such as in the day-to-day life of the administrative agency. Looking at the world through this lens, one is likely to be able to see patterns of behavior, of interpersonal dynamics, of the allocation of resources, of power that one would not otherwise see. Although people of both sexes can look through the gender lens, women are particularly likely to discover that anomalies in their own lives, things that just didn't make sense before, taken together form patterns that can be accounted for when considered from a gender perspective. They often find that experiences that seemed idiosyncratic, even "crazy," and which had led them to distrust their own senses and judgment, now make sense (Frye, 1996, p. 34). Finally able to explain experiences they had formerly chalked up to their own "hang-ups," women have often gone on to question traditional assumptions about what is "natural, . . . inevitable, appropriate, or even good" (Haslinger, 1996, p. 84) and to find that seeing certain things that go on in the world as contingent rather than inevitable leads toward the idea of changing them.

Feminists tend to see theory not as instrumental but as constitutive (Ferguson, 1984). That is, theory is not so much a tool to apply to reality "out there," the way one applies a wrench to a bolt; rather, theory brings the world into focus: It organizes, frames, and makes the world meaningful. In this sense, theory almost brings the world into being. Theory—in this case, the gender lens—organizes the world, bounding the flow of lived life into shapes and arenas and interpreting relations among human beings, their activities, and their ideas so that we can make sense of our experience and begin to question what does not fit.

The conceptual boundaries established by theory—the road map they create of the world—bring power along with them, in the sense of enablement as well as the sense of "power over." "The limits of what people can think set the limits of what they can do" (Cocks, 1989, p. 30). Thus, when we come to agreements about which considerations appropriately lie within or outside a particular area of thought (such as public administration), we also set limits on the lived experience of people who inhabit this form of life. The way we frame a theoretical conversation not only makes a certain kind of coherence possible but, if it becomes pervasive enough, establishes an orthodoxy that literally keeps us from being able to hear certain voices that have been defined as not parties to the dialogue because they raise issues that do not fit or belong. Once during a meeting of public administration theorists I heard a well-known and respected figure say that he wanted a "structured public argument" that would make certain questions off-limits—an unusually explicit declaration of a strategy by which intellectuals in disciplines (not to mention members of organizations) achieve, beyond specific conceptual wrangles, a definitional level of like-mindedness that keeps the boundaries of their consensus from being breached. But the insistence on maintaining these established boundaries is at the same time a strategy of legitimation and a strategy of suppression—a flexing of cognitive muscle that has not only conceptual but practical consequences. For example, when questions of gender or race are seen as irrelevant to public administration, many of the greatest needs and interests of people in public service—people whose lives have been shaped by their gender and/or racial identities—are eliminated from consideration. Their voices are silenced unless they are willing to speak a language in which there is no room for some of their most urgent concerns. In addition, there is the possibility that taken-for-granted ideas and theories about administrative practice may shape people's understandings about their work so that they discount their identities as women and/or people of color because there doesn't seem to be any legitimate way of taking them into account.

A feminist approach to public administration theory—at least, *this* feminist's approach—entails calling these conceptual boundaries into question and exploring their implications, which include the practical differences in access to resources and power they sustain and the perceptions of self and world they generate. I hope my analysis will stimulate people to reflect on a few of public administration's unexamined assumptions and boundaries. My aim is not to make a conclusive statement, even in the limited areas of thought with which this book deals, but to raise issues and spark discussion. Many of the topics I explore need and deserve treatment in greater depth (unhappily, this is still true nearly a decade after the first edition's publication in 1993), and some of the observations are speculative. In my view, where looking through the lens of gender will take public administration is an open question, one that is best addressed in the most inclusive dialogue possible. I only insist that it is (way past) time to have this dialogue.

The implications of my argument for public administrative practice are twofold. First, the structural nature of public administration's masculine bias means that equal opportunity strategies for advancing women's careers in public service, important though they are as a matter of sheer justice, cannot be counted on in and of themselves to change public administrative affairs. As long as we go on viewing the enterprise of administration as genderless, women will continue to face their present Hobson's choice: either to adopt a masculine administrative identity or to accept marginalization in the bureaucratic hierarchy. In either case, the intellectual assumptions, definitions of knowledge, and values that shape administrative thinking—and in turn the conditions of people's lives—are likely to remain as masculine and as disadvantageous to women as they now are.

The second implication of this exploration of public administration theory is that changes in thinking *can* effect changes in real-life circumstances: that developing an understanding of the connections between habits of thought and societal arrangements can lead human beings to take concrete actions that will change things for the better. Actually, taking concrete actions that have this sort of liberatory purpose *are* changes for the better. So are conversations that raise issues and voice previously excluded perspectives. Thus my position is that altering the composition of the public administration "choir" will do little unless its members become conscious of the need to sing different tunes from the ones currently in the repertoire, but that given the latter, much is possible.

2

"On Tap But Not on Top"

Women in the Administrative State

Ever since Woodrow Wilson wrote the first scholarly paper on public administration, practical circumstances have influenced images of administrative governance. Wilson's (1887) statement that it was "getting harder to run a constitution than to frame one" (p. 200) was made in light of new economic and political complexities facing those charged with carrying on the affairs of the nation. Today's defenses of public administration continue to be attuned to the implications of such factors as a federal system of government, a market economy, interest group politics, bureaucratic organizational form, the characteristics of fiscal and human resources, computerization, and other concrete aspects of the American administrative state in the late 20th and early 21st centuries. To do otherwise would be to risk irrelevance, a charge that theorists in an applied field are more than usually anxious to avoid.

Yet public administration theory has been curiously insensitive to the gender dimensions of political, economic, and social factors that affect public bureaucratic practices. Judging from the attention they devote to other structural and practical factors, it seems that those who write about public administrators as experts, leaders, and businesslike managers believe it is important to take the real world into account in their reflections. Against this backdrop, their failure to pay heed to gender appears to indicate that they see it as relatively insignificant in their field of observation. On the basis simply of reading arguments in defense of the administrative state, one might conclude either that there are no women in public agencies or that, although they are there, the nature of their participation, their experience of public organizational life, their career opportunities and patterns, and their problems are so little different from those of men as to have no effect—or at least none worth taking into account—on the substance of public administration from which these images are drawn.

The purpose of this chapter is to set the stage for a critique of the literature by suggesting that such is not the case. Women have been government employees now for nearly a century and a half, and from the first days of their entry into public employment they had work experiences, career opportunities, and problems unique to them. I want to raise questions about the fact of women's presence in public bureaucracies instead of taking it for granted and to argue that their experiences are both different from men's and significant in their own right. In my view, our understanding of the real world of public administration—hence any theory about it—is incomplete without taking into account the terms of women's relationships to the administrative state. I suggest that women are quintessentially "on tap" but still rarely "on top" and that this tangible circumstance is as important as any in painting a picture of public administration complete enough to serve as an adequate basis for theory. The discussion begins with a brief review of the history and current status of women in the career civil service. Then I deal with organizational realities that women face (including women in public service), which I argue are substantially different from men's. Next is a consideration of the gender dimensions of the administrative state, that is, the mutual shaping that occurs between women's lives and the dynamics of public administration. Finally, I reflect on the implication of these realities for defenses of administrative governance. My discussion aims not to speak the definitive word on its subject but to raise issues and stimulate reflection and dialogue.

Women in Public Service

Prior to the Civil War, the only federal agency that employed women was the U.S. Patent Office, according to Stephen B. Oates (1994), biographer of Clara Barton. (Oates notes that at this time there were several hundred postmistresses scattered across the country.) In 1854, Barton, who went on to fame as founder and first president of the American Red Cross, began working as a copyist in the Patent Office along with three other women. Patent Office Commissioner Charles Mason believed that women made competent and efficient copyists. Barton always maintained that she was the only one of the four who was "regularly" employed, the others simply filling in for sick husbands or fathers. Evidently Barton was so good at her job that Mason soon promoted her to "regular 'temporary' clerk" with a salary equal to that of men of similar rank, an innovation that appalled her male co-workers. Oates (1994) recounts that Barton became subject to what we would today call sexual harassment:

> When she came to her desk in the morning, they glared and whistled at her and stooped to taunts and catcalls. They also impugned her character, spreading rumors that she was a "slut" with illegitimate "negroid" children. Such behavior got her "Yankee blood" up, she said, but she refused to quit; "there was a principle involved" and she was "determined not to yield it." . . . When one malcontent complained to [Commissioner Mason] about Clara's "moral character" and insisted she be fired, the commissioner demanded proof by five o'clock that afternoon. "But understand," Mason said, "If you prove this charge, Miss Barton goes; if you fail to prove it, you go." When the deadline passed without the proof, the man went. And that put a stop to the harassment of Clara. (pp. 11–12)

With the start of the Civil War, the U.S. Department of the Treasury began to hire women in significant numbers to clip and count paper currency, replacing men who were needed as soldiers. Congress enacted legislation authorizing the hiring of women at $600 per year, or half the salary of the lowest paid male clerk. Women thus enabled the federal government to meet a critical need for more workers without straining its budget. Once inside the door, women stayed in the federal government; counting currency remained an exclusively female function for the rest of the century (Aron, 1987).

As Aron points out, the mixing of the sexes in offices was a bold experiment. Women had worked in factories since the 1820s, particularly in textile mills, where they were the majority of the workforce by 1831 (Clinton, 1984). But the women hired to work for the Treasury Department were not working-class "girls" but "ladies" who, in taking white-collar jobs, violated the notion of separated spheres—men in the public sphere, women restricted to the private—that structured middle-class social life. "Government offices were clearly men's turf. One had only to look at the spittoons that adorned every office" (Aron, 1987, p. 163). Yet for many women the concept of separated spheres had always been more political ideology than economic reality. The economic public sphere, the world of factories, mills, and stores, had included both men and women virtually from the day "work" began to move outside the household. But the liberalist idea of a political public sphere distinct from the private, when linked to widespread ideas about women's proper role, barred women from full citizenship at the same time that a burgeoning capitalist economy made use of them. The notion of separate spheres, then, served to exclude women from political benefits such as voting but not to protect them from economic exigencies. Permitting women to take a part in government, even at so lowly a level, was a significant breach in the gender-based wall between public and domestic rather than in any real barrier between government and business activity.

Women's entrance into public employment occurred on a different basis from the charity work that, although men shared it, had been considered uniquely feminine from its inception (see Chapter 6). Women invaded the male world of government employment "not because [it] required women's benign, compassionate, and caring influence, but because federal offices needed cheap labor and middle-class women needed good jobs" (Aron, 1987, p. 182). The need was such that by 1870 there were nearly 1,000 female federal employees, about 16% of the total in Washington, D.C.

Aron (1987) suggests that some of the problems that plague women workers today were evident even in the early decades of their involvement in public employment, including (as Clara Barton discovered) sexual harassment and discriminatory treatment. For example, in 1864 (only three years after women were hired in significant numbers), a special congressional committee had to look into "certain charges against the Treasury Department" that seem to have entailed male supervisors attempting to win sexual favors from their female employees. In 1869, John Ellis's *The Sights and Sounds of the Nation's Capital* commented that "the acceptance of a Government clerkship by a woman is her first step on the road to ruin" (quoted in Aron, 1987, pp. 166–167). The first annual report of the Civil Service Commission observed that the new merit system would benefit female job seekers because it would remove the necessity for them to exert political influence or resort to "importunate solicitations, especially disagreeable to women" (quoted in Aron, 1987, p. 100). As early as the decade from 1884–1894, we find evidence of discrimination in hiring: During this period, women constituted between 28% and 43% of those passing civil service examinations but only 7% to 25% of those actually hired—a disparity that reflects the exercise of discretion on the part of the appointing officer in the particular agency (quoted in Aron, 1987, pp. 109–110).

According to Harley (1990), black women were among those who applied for and received federal jobs during the 19th century; but black males held most of such higher-level positions as were "reserved for blacks in Washington, D.C. throughout the 1880–1930 period" (p. 163). Brooks-Higginbotham (1989) argues that "black women in the District [of Columbia] did not benefit from the feminization of clerical work in the late nineteenth century as did white women. . . .Racism confined the great majority to domestic service and thus presented them with fewer options than black men for upgrading their class position or working conditions" (pp. 131–132).

In the early 20th century, educated women who had become active in the settlement and municipal reform movements began to be appointed to positions in state and local governments. Hull House founder Jane Addams was appointed garbage inspector for her neighborhood after she complained repeatedly about the quality of the service. She and an assistant followed the garbage trucks to the dump, made charts of collection patterns, pushed to have landlords arrested, and argued with the contractor (Davis, 1984). Frances Kellor of College Settlement in New York investigated corrupt employment agencies for their treatment of immigrants; in 1910, the governor of New York tapped her to head the newly created Bureau of Industries and Immigration within the state Department of Labor (Fitzpatrick, 1990). In 1914, Katherine B. Davis of Philadelphia's College Settlement became the first woman to head a New York City agency when she was appointed commissioner of corrections. She promised that she would run her agency "exactly as a man would" ("Trained Social Workers Take Charge," 1914, p. 431).

In 1912, Julia Lathrop, a Hull House resident who had been active in social welfare work, was named to head the new U.S. Children's Bureau, becoming the first woman to run a federal agency. The creation of the bureau was the result of lobbying by settlement residents. Interestingly, in light of discrimination against women at the time, Lathrop used civil service regulations to fill the ranks of her bureau with women. As Robyn Muncy (1991) notes,

> The Civil Service rules—ostensibly written to assure that merit alone qualified an applicant for government jobs—explicitly allowed the heads of agencies to specify the sex of candidates for all positions. . . . Lathrop obtained permission from the Civil Service Commission to accept only female eligibles from existing civil service lists for most of her hiring. . . .Lathrop thus ensured that women dominated the Children's Bureau. . . .By March 1919, the Bureau listed only 14 men among its 169 staff members, and women outnumbered men in every occupational category except that of messenger.[1] (pp. 50–51)

World War I marked a significant change in the public sector participation of women, not only furthering the cause of suffrage but bringing increasing numbers of women into both paid and volunteer work for the war effort. The Women's Committee of the U.S. Council of National Defense coordinated a wide variety of activities on the part of women, stimulating housewives' food conservation, working with the Children's Bureau to save the lives of thousands of infants, and investigating conditions of women workers in war industries. Lemons (1973/1990) writes that "college girls worked on farms, women lawyers on exemption boards, women draftsmen [sic] in the Navy Department, and women physicians in hospitals in France" (pp. 16–17). Women demonstrated that they could do the work as well as the men they collaborated with or replaced, and new demands for equal opportunity and equal pay were heard.

The interest of feminists of the time in furthering the cause of equal opportunity employment led to the creation of the Women's Bureau in 1920, the first policy development entity in the federal government that focused specifically on the needs of women: "Women did not want an agency just to collect statistics about industrial women; they wanted a special counsel in government and continuous attention to the needs of wage-earning women. They wanted an open channel to present the problems of women, to give the women's point of view," according to Lemons (p. 27). While the creation of the bureau was cause for feminist celebration, their joy was tempered by provisions in the authorizing legislation that excluded bureau employees from a postwar bonus of $240 given to other federal workers and set the salaries of bureau statisticians at $1,800 to $2,000 per annum when statisticians in the Bureau of Labor Statistics were receiving $2,280 to $3,000 (p. 30).

During the 1920s, women were employed in government in increasing numbers, but virtually all of them were in clerical positions (Lemons, 1973/1990). Harley (1990) notes that between 1920 and 1930 "racism in the federal government began to push black women and men out of white collar job opportunities. . . .Black federal employees who maintained their positions were increasingly victimized by racially-inspired policies and practices, such as segregated offices, cafeterias, and restrooms" (p. 164). Discrimination against African Americans, public administrationists should note, was set in motion decades earlier during Woodrow Wilson's presidency and with his approval.[2]

The onset of the Depression extended overtly exclusionary practices to white women as well. Soaring unemployment rates made working women, especially those who were married, the target of efforts to restrict available jobs to men, on the theory that women worked for pin money. State and local governments passed laws barring women from public employment; they were joined by the federal government in 1932. Section 213 of the Economy Act required personnel cuts to be made by releasing "persons" whose "spouses" were also employed by the government (the original wording, deleted in committee, was *married woman* rather than *person*). Many women were forced to search desperately for alternative work, which almost always paid less; protests led to the bill's repeal in 1937 (Lemons, 1973/1990, pp. 230–231).

During World War II, women flooded into a multitude of jobs from which they had previously been excluded, and despite the postwar emphasis on domesticity and "togetherness," women's labor force participation continued to rise after the war as it had throughout the 20th century. Women constituted 26.5% of all employed workers in 1940, but their share had risen to 35% by 1960. During the same period, the percentage of female federal government workers lagged behind private sector levels but did increase from 22.7% to 25% (U.S. Bureau of the Census, 1940, 1960).

A revived women's movement beginning in the mid-1960s set in motion a new expansion in the proportion of employed women, one that apparently has yet to crest. The percentage of women who worked outside the home rose from 43.3% in 1970 to 59.8% in 1998, by which time they made up 46% of all those employed. In 1995, women comprised 43% of private sector managerial and related employees and 53% of professionals. Yet one in five of all working women held a secretarial or clerical job, a proportion that had not changed since 1950. Occupational de facto segregation by sex is still pervasive: Women still account for more than 98% of secretaries and more than 90% of professional nurses, bookkeepers, bank tellers, and housekeepers but fewer than one in 50 carpenters or auto mechanics (Roberts, 1995). Women still hold less than 5% of top management jobs (DeWitt, 1995).

By 1970, just over 33% of full-time federal government workers were women, although as yet they were heavily concentrated in lower grade levels: Only 3% of workers in Grades 13 to 15 were female and only about 1% in Grades 16 to 18 (U.S. Bureau of the Census, 1990). By 1999, women made up 44.8% of federal executive branch employees and nearly half (49.9%) of all federal white-collar workers, 39.7% of professional employees, and 43.3% of administrators. This is comparable to rates in the private sector, where in 1995, 43% of managerial and related employees and 53% of professionals were female (U.S. Bureau of the Census, 1999). In state and local governments, women made up 34.7% of full-time workers in 1973, 41% in 1980, and 44.3% in 1997 (U.S. Bureau of the Census, 1999). The proportion of women who head state agencies rose from 2% in 1964 to 22% in 1994, although women executives in state government are still clustered in arts, aging, human services, and other traditionally female areas. Women still constitute only 7% of city managers (Bowling & Wright, 1998).

The proportion of women at middle and upper levels of the federal civil service has continued to increase, while at lower levels it has declined for white women and risen sharply for nonwhites. In 1998, 18.9% of federal employees at GS Grades 14 and 15 were white women, up from 8.9% in 1986. The percentage of minority women at this level rose from 1.9% in 1986 to 5.6% by 1998. In 1986, white women made up 47.2% of employees at Grades 1 through 4, with minority women constituting 29.4%; by 1998, the proportion of white women had declined to 36.8%, but strikingly, the percentage of minority women had risen to 62.8%. The absolute number of employees at the lower grades fell from 282,794 in 1986 to 111,700 in 1998; in the process, it appears that more women of color than white women remained stuck at lower grade levels. At the top ranks of the federal government, white women made up 18.3% of the Senior Executive Service by 1998, while 3.9% were minority women and 8.5% minority men (U.S. Office of Personnel Management, 1998,

2000). Although these figures reflect progress, women of all races are still not adequately represented in the ranks of federal managers in comparison to their proportions in the U.S. population as a whole.

A 1988 Hudson Institute report identified the continued rise in the proportion of women workers as one of three important demographic issues facing federal managers at the end of the 20th century. In assessing the significance of this continuing trend for personnel policies and practices, the report acknowledged the structural disparity between the life circumstances of men and those of women and the likely influence of this disparity on policy decision making:

> Because Federal women, like most women within society, will continue to have the lion's share of the household and family responsibilities in addition to their jobs, there is little doubt that such current issues as day-care, benefit reforms, more flexible hours of work, leave time, and other policies will continue to be a source of debate. As women rise within the Federal bureaucracy to policymaking positions they are likely, within the limits of the law, to reinterpret Federal policies regarding work and families and to promote more family-oriented policies. (Hudson Institute, 1988, pp. 26–27)

Interestingly, while the report notes that the federal government is a leader in providing day-care services at the work site, it argues that "child care benefits are of no value to the majority of Federal employees" and suggests a "cafeteria" approach that might require employees needing day care to trade off other benefits in return. One wonders whether the institute would encourage local governments to require taxpaying families with children to trade off fire protection or garbage collection for public education.[3]

Women's Organizational Reality

Researchers who want to defend themselves against the charge of neglecting women's presence in public administration might offer the argument that organizations are organizations and women are simply some of the workers in them—that women's experiences in organizations as well as the general circumstances of their lives reflect no significant differences from men's. This would be a curious position to take in a culture that expends as much energy as ours does on seeing to it that gender distinctions are maintained (Epstein, 1988). Nevertheless, it may be helpful to the general cause of promoting public administration theorists' attention to gender to reflect briefly on some of the dimensions of women's organizational and life circumstances as various observers have noted them. My assumption is that if roughly half the inhabitants of the realm of public administration are having experiences that are not only not taken into account by theories but are actually at odds with them, then it is time to reexamine the bases of these arguments.

Sheppard (1989) notes the practical difficulty in bringing to light the disparity between women's and men's organizational realities:

> Under the tremendous pressures for acceptance and conformity necessary to success at work in our social world, which are heightened greatly for women in a male-dominated environment, the differences in the ways in which women and men may formulate their experiences are generally not readily apparent. While women continue to demonstrate their capacity for succeeding at "men's work" and often excelling at it, we are realizing that under the surface of achievement, women are experiencing a work reality that differs from that of men in many ways. (p. 141)

According to Sheppard, to consider organizational structures as objective and neutral when men's customary practices and values still so clearly pervade them is to wear ideological blinders. Her research shows that both men and women associate issues of sex and gender in organizations with femaleness but not with maleness. The latter is simply not considered remarkable because it blends so easily with standard organizational processes. Sheppard notes that sometimes women do experience stereotypically male behavior as a problem, but for them to address it openly requires such a fundamental challenge to prevailing norms that women often instead redefine problematic situations either by choosing to ignore tensions and ambiguities or by focusing on their own identities—in other words, by seeing their own behavior and perceptions rather than men's as the source of the particular difficulty. For this reason, research that relies on self-reporting, particularly that in which women are found to perceive little dissonance between themselves and prevailing practices, must be interpreted with caution.

The problem for women members of organizations is how to manage their femaleness. Because expectations (widely shared by both women and men) about how managers and leaders will behave conform to expectations of male but not of female behavior, women must make deliberate efforts to balance conflicting roles. "Without constant vigilance regarding gender (and sexual) self-presentation, these women perceive that they run the risk of not being taken seriously, not being heard, and not receiving information" (Sheppard, 1989, p. 145). Most try to blend in—that is, present a feminine appearance but behave in a businesslike (stereotypically masculine) manner. According to Bem (1994),

> The problem for women. . . is not simply that they are different from men, whether biologically or in some other way. The problem . . . . is that they are different from men in a social world that disguises what are really just male standards or norms as gender-neutral principles. . . . If we want to understand gender inequality it is much more important to shift from an analysis of difference per se to an analysis of the ways in which the social structure privileges some people's differences at the expense of others'. (pp. B1–B2)

In other words, while much gender-oriented research has documented perceived differences in male and female behavior as well as men's and women's expectations about how each sex will behave in particular situations, relatively little thought has been given to what difference these differences make: what they imply for women's careers and organizational experiences versus those of men. When Rochelle (Rocky) Jones, one of the first women to join the New York City fire department, passed the lieutenant's exam in 1994, she was told that by becoming an officer she would no longer be one of the guys. Her response: "I was never one of them." Jones observed that 20 years after the fire department started hiring females, women were still writing the fire department saying they wanted to be the first women firefighters in New York, reflecting the relative invisibility of a scattering of women in a still overwhelmingly male occupation (Hoffman, 1999, p. A22).

Gutek's (1989) literature review addresses another dimension of women's organizational reality. Studies show that, in general, women are associated with the status of sex object—with being, regardless of context, sexual beings who "naturally" evoke sexual overtures from men:

> In a 32-nation study of sex stereotypes, the characteristics of sexy, affectionate, and attractive were associated with femaleness. . . . There is no strongly held comparable belief about men. . . . The stereotype of men revolves around the dimension of competence and activity. It includes the belief that men are rational, analytic, assertive, tough, good at maths [sic] and science, competitive, and make good leaders . . . the perfect picture of asexuality. (Gutek, 1989, pp. 59–60)

Thus women in organizations have the additional problem of trying to appear feminine without triggering "natural" sexual reactions in men. If they do trigger such responses, women rather than men are customarily assumed to be at fault.

Culturally feminine characteristics do not fit the Weberian model of bureaucratic organization, which emphasizes instrumental rationality and official relations and excludes feeling. Pringle (1989) argues that Weber's idea of rationality, because it depends on excluding the personal, the sexual, and the feminine, can be read as a gloss on organizational masculinity. She suggests that, although Weber saw the bureaucratic order of the modern world as a replacement for traditional patriarchy, one can see bureaucracy instead as a new form of patriarchy: "The apparent neutrality of rules and goals disguises the class and gender interests" that bureaucracy serves (p. 161). Although obviously no actual bureaucracy fits Weber's ideal type exactly, our commonsense understanding of what an organization is supposed to be—a rational instrument for the efficient accomplishment of objectives—makes sexual emotion a taboo; as the people whose sex in organizations is problematic, women become associated with that which is forbidden, hence repressed. Milwid (1990), for example, notes that both men and women professionals in organizations seek to deny the existence of sexual harassment. Nevertheless, her research suggested that such incidents are widespread and that most go unreported, frequently because women are apt to blame themselves when men at work make overtures. Hale and Kelly (1989) found that 48% of female federal employees had experienced sexual harassment, with "severe" harassment, such as pressure for sexual favors, twice as common as "less severe" (jokes, suggestive remarks).

Wells's (1973) study of the covert power of gender in organizations expresses the hidden sexual dimension of organizational reality in terms of a double bind that women's presence places on men:

> If [the male manager] accepts women as managers, he has to accept as OK-for-a-manager the emotions he has repressed in himself; if he accepts the prescribed unemotional manager's role, he can't accept women (the feminine) as managers. . . .
>
> The male role requires that women be taken care of, not fought. So, many men feel locked into another double-bind: if he's a man as prescribed, he cannot relate to a woman on an equal basis; if he's his own person, relating as an equal to a woman, he risks being seen by other men as "not much of a man"—or manager either. (p. 61)

Like women, then, men have to repress or deny aspects of themselves to function in organizations. Ferguson (1984) argues that the fact that most organizational men are in subordinate positions within the hierarchical structure of the bureaucracy requires them to behave in ways that outside the organization would be considered stereotypically feminine. For example, in general, men in organizations must cater to their superiors, avoid confrontation with them, and become sensitive to their idiosyncrasies. Their interest in being seen as real men, however, works to keep them from perceiving their behavior as consistent with femininity. Kanter (1977) suggests that what looks like preference for masculinity in organizations is actually preference for power and that leadership styles are correlated not with gender but with the power of the position a particular leader holds. In her view, for example, the bossiness of women supervisors about which both male and female employees complain is not a feminine trait but the behavior of someone who has significant responsibility but little real power. Because in actuality most top leaders in organizations are men, however, organizational members continue to associate effective leadership with masculinity and to assume that a woman's problematic behavior has to do with her gender rather than her subordinate place in the structure or the power dynamics of the organization.

Glass Ceilings, Glass Walls

Perhaps the most undeniable aspect of women's different organizational reality is their continued lack of access to high-ranking positions. A recent study found that among 12,997 officers at the nation's 500 largest corporations, only 10% were women. Among the 2,500 "top earners" in these companies, only 2% were female. More than 100 companies, including Exxon, Nynex, and Whirlpool, had no women in top jobs (Dobrzynski, 1996, p. C2). Looking just at the five highest titles (chief executive officer, chairman, vice chairman, president, and chief operating officer) in *Fortune* 500 companies, in 1998 women made up less than 1% (Powell, 1999, p. 329). "In 1978 . . . there were two women heading Fortune 1000 companies; in 1994 there were also two; in August of 1996 . . . there were four" (Valian, 1998, p. 191). Stroh and Reilly (1999) comment that gender segregation can be found throughout the management hierarchy, "up to and including boards of directors and chief executive officers. For example, women board members were more likely to be placed on public affairs committees, and men on compensation, executive, and finance committees" (p. 312). Virtually all the women who have made it to the top ranks are white (DeWitt, 1995, p. B14). White women have made somewhat greater strides into middle management, where they now hold about 40% of the positions, but blacks have done markedly worse: Black women still make up only about 5% and black men 4%.

In the federal government, women made up 39.7% of professionals and 43.3% of administrators in 1999 (U.S. Office of Personnel Management, 2000, p. 50). At the top of the federal bureaucracy, by 1998 women constituted 22.2% of the Senior Executive Service, up from 5.1% in 1979 (Dolan, 2000; U.S. Office of Personnel Management, 1998). In 1999, women made up 29.4% of employees in Grades 13 through 15 (a 212.4% increase in the ratio from 1986), 44.2% in Grades 9 through 12 (up 22.9%), 68.5% in Grades 5 through 8 (off 17.4%), and 68.8% in Grades 1 through 4, a two-thirds decline in the proportion of women since 1986 (U.S. Office of Personnel Management, 2000, pp. 28, 50). Interestingly, in middle management the ratios of women in private and federal government organizations are roughly comparable, although it might be expected that public employers would do better. At the top levels, they have indeed done better, with the ratio of women in the SES about double that of women in the upper echelons of corporate America. A study of one federal agency found that the sex of applicants for SES positions did influence promotion decisions. Progress in this area, the researchers commented, "may have been due to the federal government's special promotion procedures in addition to its strong commitment to equal opportunity employment." The government's promotion practices "enable identification of improperly made decisions, thereby making decision makers accountable for how promotion decisions are made" (Powell, 1999, pp. 336–337).

In state and local governments in 1997, women made up 33.4% of officials and administrators (up from 29.1% in 1987) and 53.1% of professionals (up from 48.1%) (U.S. Bureau of the Census, 1999). A study released in 1992 found that the number of women in senior posts in state and local governments (department heads, division chiefs, deputies and examiners) ranged from 13.9% in Hawaii to 38.5% in Louisiana. In the typical state or local government, minority women made up only 5.1% of top managers ("Few Women," 1992, p. A8).

Recent research on employment patterns in municipal governments found the existence of "glass walls," or the concentration of women in particular agencies. Using previously unavailable data from the U.S. Equal Opportunity Employment Commission to examine employment patterns in cities with between 250 and 15,000 employees, the researchers concluded that proportions of women in administrative and professional jobs in municipal agencies between 1986 and 1993 depended significantly on the nature of the work. In general, they found that the municipal government workforce is strikingly segregated by sex. In departments that handled streets, sewers, utilities, roads, fire, and police, women were markedly underrepresented as administrators, whereas in community development, parks, and corrections about one-third of cities had at least 30% females in administrative jobs. In contrast, women were markedly overrepresented in welfare work (median of 60%), and hospital administrative jobs (median of 64%). In the case of professionals, the researchers comment, "Gender-based occupational segregation is the norm among professional municipal workforces in streets and highways, sanitation and sewage, and utilities and transportation" as, indeed, it is in the case of municipal hospitals, where the typical city's professional workforce is 90% female, or health and welfare agencies, where professionals are about three-quarters female in the typical city (Miller, Kerr, & Reid, 1999, p. 224).

Not surprising, in a 1994 Women's Bureau study that included both nonsystematic and random samples of working women, nearly half of respondents said they were not being paid what they deserved (Lewin, 1994, p. 8). The study found that women earned 71 cents for every dollar earned by men, up from 61 cents in 1978. Most of the improvement in this ratio was the result of declines in men's average earnings rather than increases in women's pay. Roos and Gatta (1999) note that, after reaching a high in 1993, the median weekly earnings ratio between men and women began to decline. Studies indicate that disparities between men's and women's pay cannot be accounted for fully by the types of jobs held or levels of education and experience. Women who have amassed as much "human capital" as men still have somewhat lower wages. As Valian (1998) notes, even though the disparity between comparably educated and experienced men and women is small, "it should not have existed at all" (p. 193). A study of the career progression of male and female managers at 20 *Fortune* 500 companies found that "female managers and professionals . . . had done 'all the right stuff.'" They had comparable education, had stayed in the workforce, had moved for career reasons as often as the men had, and were generally less encumbered by family than the men were. Yet their salaries lagged behind those of the men. The researchers commented, "Corporate America has run out of explanations that attribute women's career patterns to women's own behavior. It is time for corporations to take a closer look at their own behavior" (Stroh, Brett, & Reilly, 1992, pp. 257–258).

A three-year study of African American, Asian American, and Hispanic women at 30 large U.S. companies found that minority women managers and professionals are earning less than their white and male counterparts, and that black and Hispanic women have actually seen the gap widen over the past 5 years. In 1998, Hispanic women managers made only 60% of white male managers' salaries, compared to 70% in 1993. A striking finding was that the diversity programs of large companies benefit white women much more than minority women. "We were moving women, but we were basically moving white women," commented Roberta Gutman, vice-president and director for global diversity at Motorola (quoted in Abelson, 1999, p. C4).

According to the federal glass ceiling report (U.S. Glass Ceiling Commission, 1995), many middle- and upper-level white male managers feel threatened by increases in minority and female employment in the managerial ranks. They tend to interpret such changes as a direct challenge to their own chances for advancement. The report found that while top executives understand the need for a diverse workforce in a global economy, middle managers steer women to non-career-track jobs in personnel and public relations. One white male manager commented somewhat defensively, "What's important is comfort, chemistry.... When we find minorities and women who think like we do, we snatch them up" (quoted in Kilborn, 1995, p. C22).

One observer forecasts that as more women become conscious of the realities of their organizational lives their discontent will rise (Laws, 1976); whether that discontent will simply lead to apathy in the face of seemingly insurmountable barriers or can be turned to more positive change efforts is an open question. Research indicates that women are much more likely than men to attribute women's organizational disadvantage to persistent gender stereotypes. A 1996 report found that 52% of top corporate women surveyed put "male stereotyping and preconceptions of women" at the top of their list of barriers to advancement, in contrast to just 25% of the male chief executives who ranked this first. Male CEOs, in contrast, rated women's lack of management experience as the most important barrier. The president of the firm that conducted the study observed that, on the whole, women managers discount the so-called pipeline theory: "Most women do not believe that it's simply a matter of time" (quoted in Dobrzynsky, 1996, p. C2). Such studies indicate that women are fully aware of the organizational discrimination they still face, although the risks that accompany any overt action to combat this reality tend to work against concerted efforts.

Who's Minding the Kids?

Standard organizational and professional career patterns as well as the ongoing fabric of organizational life depend on the existence of someone (in stereotype, a wife) who takes care of household and child-care responsibilities. Women in the labor force, attempting to shoulder their domestic obligations and hold down paid jobs at the same time, work a double shift that is another factor in their different organizational reality. Because the American political economy counts on women as a group to handle these societal necessities irrespective of their individual inclination to do so, the arrangement constitutes oppression of women. Those who doubt the structural nature of women's disproportionate domestic burden might try imagining what would happen to organizational routines if one day all married employed women—or those who are unemployed because their small children "need someone at home"—freely decided that they would no longer carry more than half the responsibility for housework and child care. Working women's double shift not only takes its toll in 18-hour days and stress-related illness, it also makes it difficult for women to meet employer expectations that family responsibilities will not interfere with work obligations and thus to keep up with (or get on) the fast track to the upper echelons of the organization. These tensions, or their prospect, in fact lead many women to deal with the prospect of a double burden of job and family responsibilities by rejecting marriage and childbearing. Hale and Kelly's (1989) survey of state employees in Arizona, California, Utah, and Texas found that the living situations and domestic responsibilities of the male and female respondents were significantly different:

> Women are more likely to be divorced or never married, to be living alone, and without dependents. . . . Women are more likely than men to regard childbearing, child rearing, and household tasks as having interfered with their careers and . . . many apparently have resolved the traditional public/private role conflicts they face by not having a traditional family life. These women have not solved the historic dilemma of private/public role conflict; they have avoided it. Domestic responsibilities appear to constrain the career development of women more than men. (p. 144)

King (1992) found a similar pattern in her study of state managers in Colorado: 88% of the men in her sample were married in contrast to 59% of the women. Hale and Kelly (1989) also note that, despite the fact that the women in their study had changed jobs within the bureaucracy at a faster rate and at younger ages than the male respondents had, the women were still paid from $3,000 to $5,000 less than the men and, on average, supervised fewer employees.

Sherley Williams calls the equal sharing of family responsibilities between men and women "the great revolution that never happened" (quoted in Okin, 1989, p. 4). Employed men do an average of 18.2 hours of housework a week. This represents just over a third of all the housework done by the couple. Men's housework hours are divided evenly between "female" and "male" chores, whereas women's housework is spent mostly on female chores (Lennon & Rosenfeld, 1994). Male chores are thought to include yard work and auto maintenance, female chores to encompass meal preparation, dishes, washing and ironing, cleaning house, and shopping (Blair & Lichter, 1991). Most research studies have concluded that the amount of housework men do is affected neither by whether their wives work outside the home nor by the level of wives' salaries. Study after study has found that both men and women continue to define household work as "women's work." The sexes agree that men should bear more of the breadwinning responsibility than women, whereas women should be more responsible for family work and child care (Major, 1993). Even among couples where both hold professional jobs and whose salaries are relatively equal, housework is not shared equally. Despite this disparity, women declared themselves to be satisfied with the existing division of labor and were relatively critical of their own performance in the domestic sphere, in comparison to non-employed wives and mothers (Biernat & Wortman, 1991). The persistence of these beliefs means that, in general, neither women nor men perceive the unequal division of household work as unfair, even though employed wives may do two or three times as much housework and child care as their husbands:

> Women's greater responsibility for family tasks and child care reflects and helps to perpetuate social norms and values, and limits women's equal participation in the paid labor force. Women's unequal participation in the paid labor force in turn affects their perceptions of what they are entitled to at home. Thus, rather than being "separate

spheres," justice in the workplace and justice in the family are closely connected. (Major 1993, p. 156)

Okin (1989) argues that during their developing years women "are set up for vulnerability" to exploitation in the marital relationship because they internalize society's expectation that they will be the primary child rearers (p. 138). Okin says that because the world of business (I would add government) is still structured around the assumption that employees are people who have wives at home and can thus work full time (or more), "to the extent that wives work part-time or intermittently, their own career potential atrophies" (p. 156). Okin holds that "the major reason that husbands and other heterosexual men living with wage-working women are not doing more housework is that they do not want to, and are able, to a very large extent, to enforce their wills" (p. 153). Actually, if the research cited above is sound, not much enforcement is necessary because women have internalized the idea that housework is primarily up to them; therefore they are likely, even when they work full-time, not to see as unfair the disproportionate share they perform in comparison to their husbands.

Thus, because gender stereotypes make women anomalies in the organizational context and because they suffer under economic arrangements that shore up accepted bureaucratic practices, women's organizational reality is significantly different from men's. On the one hand, women do not fit well within existing organizations, government or business, in which masculine behavior is congruent with general organizational expectations while women's is not. On the other hand, the standard procedures of these organizations depend on women to provide support for the careers of male managers by shouldering not only most domestic responsibilities but also much of the routine, poorly paid, lower-level organizational work. Far more women experience organizational reality both in the administrative state and in corporations as data entry clerks, secretaries, bookkeepers, and maintenance workers than as vice presidents or bureau chiefs. Lewis calls clerical work the "quintessential female occupation" in the federal civil service (quoted in Hale & Kelly, 1989, p. 12). In addition, Hale and Kelly (1989) point out that in both state and federal governments the career ladders for female-dominated positions have lower entry levels, less mobility across grade levels, and lower top levels. Women now make up slightly more than half the labor force, but it is not the top half. Most women develop their view of the organization sitting in the clerical bull pen at the bottom of the bureaucratic pyramid and/or dashing back and forth between home and work in a desperate effort to meet clashing expectations.

Women and the Administrative State

Most of the features of women's organizational reality can be found equally in the business and government sectors. But as public administration theorists are fond of noting, public and business organizations are alike in all unimportant respects. In light of the research presented above, perhaps not *all* the ways in which government agencies and profit-making businesses are alike are unimportant. It remains true, however, that the differences between them are significant. Yet those that have to do with gender are rarely if ever taken into account.

Theorists who regard public organizations as unique do so because they view the actions of public agencies as governance, a view that can be traced to Dwight Waldo's (1948) introduction of the idea of "the administrative state" into the literature. The literature defending the administrative state treats bureaucratic decision making as in need of justification precisely because it constitutes a form of governance, that is, the exercise of legitimate power. Yet many of the implications of the concept "administrative state" have been imperfectly explored. For example, Van Riper's (1983) widely cited list of characteristics of the administrative state includes none that frankly acknowledges politics, let alone power, as defining qualities of a state. Recently, the importance of administrative power has been argued by Holden (1996), but as Holden himself notes, power continues to be widely ignored by public administration scholars, even though among political theorists power plays a central part in defining the notion of a "state."

According to Poggi (1978, p. 1), a state asserts monopoly over the "business of rule," or the giving of commands to society at large, a function that in classical liberal thought distinguishes it from the rest of society. The modern state is a complex assortment of legislative, judicial, and administrative entities, but the bulk of its actions consists of directives of varying specificity and their implementation, made and carried out by a hierarchy of offices, the holders of which have mastered knowledge of applicable laws and the intellectual techniques for interpreting them—who are, in fact, administrators exercising discretionary authority (Poggi, 1990).

Classical liberal thought puts great emphasis on maintaining the state's clear boundaries, in order to reserve a space of liberty for individual preferences and actions. Yet as Mitchell (1991) observes, "producing and maintaining the distinction between state and society is itself a mechanism that generates resources of power" (p. 90). Mitchell argues that contemporary politics does not consist of policy formation on one side of the divide and policy impact on the other but, rather, of "the producing and reproducing of this line of difference" (p. 95; see also Honig, 1993). This critical perspective focuses our attention on the energy expended on maintaining the separation between state and society, rather than simply taking it for granted.

Applying this thinking to public administration—that is, questioning the insistence on a phenomenon called *the administrative state* wholly separate from something called the private sphere—we must ask what is obscured as a result of constructing and defending this firm boundary. The public-private distinction has served historically to maintain the perception that there is a clear line between government and business and to justify a realm in which "man" is protected from government interference in his activities. At the same time, the public-private dichotomy has been used to distinguish the household from *both* government and business activities. Neither distinction has served women well; rather, both have covered up women's needs and made them theoretical anomalies. The terms in which the administrative state's legitimacy is defended, which this book explores, bring these incongruities into sharper focus.

Much of the recent attention paid in the literature to the administrative state comes from the need to combat bureaucrat bashing by making what public administrators do seem special and to improve the bureaucrat's image. Regardless of intentions, however, one of the major results of a clear *theoretical* boundary around the administrative state is to hide its *practical* dependence on women's domestic work and its reach into the most private aspects of women's lives.

Since ancient times, political philosophers have glorified the state by contrasting it with the household. Aristotle praised the *polis* as an end in itself—as the site of political dialogue and debate that were uniquely human. In his view, because "man" is a political animal (that is, politics is a defining human activity), the *polis* is higher in the overall scheme of things than household activities necessary to human existence (Aristotle, 1981). The essence of politics, in other words, is to rise above necessity (Arendt, 1958). A similar distinction was made by Machiavelli, who conceived of statecraft as the mastery of fate: Political virtue (from *vir*, man) consists in achieving control over matter (from *mater*, mother)—over an explicitly female *fortuna* (Pitkin, 1984). Here again, affairs of state are seen as separate from and superior to the concerns assigned to women. Liberal philosophy also drew a sharp line, this time between the "natural" authority of the male in the family and political authority, which rests on consent. For Locke, the chief end of government was to protect individual property rights, but to avoid extending these rights to women and thus threaten the entire social order, he postulated the natural inferiority of women based on the burdens of childbearing (Clark, 1979). Rousseau's ideal state is dependent on the existence of the home as a refuge to which the male citizen can retreat from the demands of public life to have his physical and emotional needs met by his woman (Lange, 1979).

The revolutionary eras in America and France offer examples of the deliberate ordering of the public sphere at the expense of women. In America, founding father John Adams replied with a verbal pat on the head to his wife Abigail's admonition to "remember the ladies" when designing the new government. But Abigail Adams knew that she had raised a serious and potentially threatening question. To a male colleague, John Adams voiced anxieties that show that he, too, regarded his wife's question as weighty:

> How . . . does the right arise in the majority to govern the minority, against their will? Whence arises the right of the men to govern the women, without their consent? . . . You will say, because their delicacy renders them unfit for practice and experience in the great business of life . . . as well as the arduous cares of state. . . . True. But will not these reasons apply to others? Depend upon it, Sir, it is dangerous to open so fruitful a source of controversy. . . . New claims will arise; women will demand a vote; . . . and every man who has not a farthing, will demand an equal voice with any other, in all acts of state. (quoted in Rossi, 1973, pp. 10–15)

Landes's (1988) study of the development of public space in prerevolutionary France offers another clear example of the deliberate ordering of public and domestic spheres at the expense of women. Under monarchical rule in 18th-century France, the institution of the salon offered the only space where men and women could converse about public affairs. Hosted by women, salons provided the means whereby men learned the style, language, and art necessary to operate in public and served as the arena within which important issues were discussed. Landes argues that men, "feminized" by the king's absolute power, came to see women's role in the political dialogue of the salons as analogous to the kings' monopoly over the terms of political life. Over time, men came to see silencing women and banishing them from an expanding public space as necessary to a challenge to monarchy.

Landes (1988) suggests that women, once expelled from public space, violate the code of political behavior when they attempt to reshape public language in order to make it possible to express certain issues. Seen as unutterably different, women can only give voice to what are regarded as partial concerns; they cannot join in what men believe to be the universal discourse of the public sphere. One small but significant indication of the masculinity of the public sphere and its discourse is that, in contrast to the respect accorded *public man*, since time immemorial the term *public woman* has had the connotation "prostitute."

Reconstructing our idea of the public—hence of public administration—involves questioning the boundaries we have drawn around the administrative state, which have defined women out and now leave them struggling with whether to try to "become men" in order to participate. For one thing, we must begin to question the uniqueness of some of the state's supposedly unique characteristics. For example, Franzway, Court, and Connell (1989) observe that the state is neither the only institutionalization of power nor even its only legitimate holder. The family is also a locus of power relations, and parents exercise legitimate force (short of real injury) on their children. They also note that, far from holding itself aloof from domestic issues, the administrative state develops and implements policies, such as those on divorce, birth control, and abortion, that affect our most intimate behaviors. Epstein (1988) argues that the terms of many public policies, such as protective labor laws and the prohibition on women in combat, far from simply *reflecting* gender distinctions in society actually maintain and reinforce them, including ones that disadvantage women. Franzway et al. (1989) note,

> The state is not outside society. . . . Gender relations form a large-scale structure, embracing all social institutions in particular ways. . . . The state participates in this dynamic on the same footing as any other institution (for instance reflecting the overall changes in women's employment in the last generation). . . . The state sets limits to the use of violence, protects property, criminalises stigmatized sexuality, embodies masculine hierarchy. . . . The state takes a prominent part in constituting gender categories (the homosexual, the prostitute, the housewife, the family man) and regulating the relationships among them by policy and policing. (p. 52)

Like other liberalist views of the state, public administration's defense of the administrative state depends on the state's faithful adherence to the public interest, broadly understood. From this perspective, the thing that sets public administrators apart is their commitment to the common good ahead of their own self-interests. Such an understanding turns real (not abstract) public administrators into a class set apart from the people at large by its ability to rise above self-interest into the realm of universalized concerns. Although contemporary theorists have ostensibly discarded Woodrow Wilson's politics-administration dichotomy and have acknowledged the inherently political character of bureaucrats' discretionary judgments, most have yet to consider whether a pursuit that so assiduously denies the gender (as well as the race and class) dynamics of its development can be trusted to be able to tell the partial from the universal. Although the occasional theorist addresses the administrative state's role in tending the dynamics of advanced capitalism and most acknowledge its unavoidable entanglement in interest group politics, its implication in the construction and maintenance of gender distinctions—most of which are invidious for women—has yet to be explored. Evidently, where *sexual* politics are concerned, the politics-administration dichotomy still guides thinking in public administration.

Conclusion

While public administration scholars overwhelmingly acknowledge that the field is an applied one and debate ways of making their research more useful to practitioners, one aspect of the real world of public administration has gone relatively unnoticed—the dynamics of gender in public organizational life. Since women first entered government work in the mid-19th century, their experience of life in public agencies has been fundamentally different from men's. Women have been paid less, done a disproportionate share of the routine work, struggled with the question of how to accommodate themselves to organizational practices defined by men, brooded over how to turn aside men's advances without losing their jobs, and fought to balance work demands with what was expected of them—what they expected of themselves—on the domestic front. Those who have made it to the middle ranks find themselves bumping up against a glass ceiling that keeps a disproportionate number of women from top positions. In subsequent chapters, I explore some of the ramifications of women's different organizational reality and our failure to take it into account in constructing images of professional expertise, leadership, and management on which we rely in justifying the exercise of administrative power in a representative democracy.

Notes

1. Press coverage of Lathrop's selection included bits of humor occasioned by her sex. An article in *The Survey* commented, "The head of a bureau of the federal government is called a 'chief' [and addressed in writing] as 'Dear Mr. Chief.' Consequently official Washington was thrown into consternation at the announcement that Julia Lathrop had been placed in charge of the new children's bureau, for there seemed no escape from the salutation 'Dear Miss Chief'" ("Immediate Work," 1912, p. 189).

2. Wilson defended the segregation of African-American civil servants as a move to protect them from harassment. In response to a letter of protest from Oswald Garrison Villard, *New York Evening Post* editor and grandson of abolitionist William Lloyd Garrison, Wilson commented,

> It is true that the segregation of the colored employees in the several departments was begun upon the initiative and at the suggestion of several of the heads of departments, but as much in the interest of the negroes as for any other reason, with the approval of some of the most influential negroes I know, and with the idea that the friction, or rather the discontent and uneasiness, which had prevailed in many of the departments would thereby be removed. . . . My own feeling is, by putting certain bureaus and sections of the service in the charge of negroes we are rendering them more safe in their possession of office and less likely to be discriminated against. (quoted in Baker, 1931/1968, p. 221)

3. Among state and local employees in 1987, approximately 74% received free parking as a benefit, but only 2% got child care (Peterson, 1992).

3

"Sharpening a Knife Cleverly"
The Dilemma of Expertise

One of the most pervasive topics in public administration theory is the expertise of public administrators. Practitioners and scholars argue that competence in the art of governance entitles public administrators to a certain measure of power in the fulfillment of their responsibilities. Debate centers not on this fundamental claim but on relatively secondary questions like the specific nature of the expertise, or whether it makes sense logically or strategically to consider public administration a profession.

For example, Morgan (1990) asks "What particular competence do and/or should public administrators possess in their exercise of authority?" rather than "Does expertise justify authority?" (p. 70). The "Blacksburg Manifesto" argues that whether or not we call public administration a profession, what really matters is recognition of its "truly distinctive claim to status . . . a claim of competence in the maintenance of (1) the Agency Perspective; (2) the broadest possible public interest; and (3) the constitutional governance process" (Wamsley et al., 1990, pp. 47, 39). Pugh (1989) observes—in a piece generally critical of professional status for public administration—that "the reconciliation of traditional democratic values and the need for competent expertise in the governance process is a fundamental puzzle piece in public administration's search for reasonableness" (p. 5). Cigler (1990) sees a "paradox of professionalization" in public administration: The more we try to professionalize the lower we sink in public esteem. Nevertheless, she calls on public servants to "be more proactive in lobbying for the broad public interest" rather than urging them to question the extent to which competence entitles them to power (p. 649).

While some writers maintain a certain level of skepticism about the virtues of professional status for public administration, others seek to mold the idea of professionalism in order to put it to the service of public administration's need for legitimacy. For example, Stever (1988) rejects the traditional professional model on the grounds that public administrators cannot claim exclusive control over their work; nevertheless, he offers a strategy for the professionalization of public administration, a project that in his view includes recognition of its "cruciality" and the acquisition of a "mystique" (pp. 171ff.). Nalbandian (1990) emphasizes the "rational and analytic problem-solving orientation" of local government professionals, without which they seem "hardly distinguishable from the politician" (p. 659). Green, Keller, and Wamsley (1993) suggest that the notion of professionalism in public service needs to expand beyond technical skills to "moral insight and judgment" and "integrity and commitment in institutional missions" (p. 522). Similarly, DeHoog and Whitaker (1993) see expertise as the central characteristic of public sector professionalism but argue that democratic values and an ethic of responsibility are equally important. Yet Sherwood (1997) argues that technical expertise is what distinguishes administrators from others in public service; therefore it can never entirely be dispensed with in our ideas of professionalism. Kearny and Sinha (1988) offer perhaps the most ardent defense of professional expertise in public administration: "[We agree] with such notables as Aristotle, John Stuart Mill, Woodrow Wilson, and Max Weber that the preservation of a democratic system depends upon the competence of experts in government. . . . The expanded role of the professional administrator has benefitted bureaucratic responsiveness" (p. 571). Their prescription is underscored by Barrileaux, Feiock, and Crew (1992), whose 50-state study found that "administrative professionalism [encompassing expertise, information processing, innovativeness, and efficiency], political neutrality and representativeness are generally viewed as hallmarks of good administration" (p. 17).

As the above review suggests, the substance of the public administrator's expertise is, in theory, wide ranging. It appears to include specialized (scientific, technical, and/or managerial) knowledge, analytical and problem-solving skills, the ability to see the longer view and the bigger picture, and other cognitive abilities, but also normative ones such as an especially acute understanding of the constitutional governance process or what constitutes the public interest in particular situations. This chapter deals with technical and scientific expertise; subsequent chapters address managerial and normative competencies.

There are four aspects of professional expertise in public administration that contain gender dilemmas: its claim of scientific objectivity, its quest for autonomy, the hierarchical nature of the authority it seeks, and its implicit norm of brotherhood. In considering these points, my aim is to show that each one depends on the assertion of various culturally masculine qualities and values and the disparagement of feminine ones and assumes a social order that disadvantages women. I suggest that current images of expertise are problematic because they encourage us to perceive the practice of public administration in ways that, although we tend to see them as neutral or universal, are actually gender biased and support concrete discrimination against women. The chapter concludes with a brief discussion of the paradoxes that women and the profession as a whole face as a result of arguments for public administration's legitimacy based on administrative expertise.

Objective Expertise

Objectivity and neutrality have been cited ever since Woodrow Wilson and Frank Goodnow as major bases for the legitimacy of administrative experts in a constitutional democracy. In order to "run a constitution," Wilson (1887) argued, the "eminently practical science of [public] administration" must look to wherever expert methods are practiced, whether it be the business world or European monarchy (pp. 200, 197). The reason we need not worry about borrowing techniques from these seemingly alien realms is because expert methods themselves are neutral. In a famous metaphor, Wilson maintains that "if I see a murderous fellow sharpening a knife cleverly, I can borrow his way of sharpening the knife without borrowing his probable intention to commit murder with it; and so, if I see a monarchist dyed in the wool managing a public bureau well, I can learn his business methods without changing one of my republican spots" (p. 220).

Wilson's argument is only the most familiar expression of a theme that pervaded the Progressive reform movement: the need to rescue government from bias, corruption, and bossism by turning it over to educated, neutral experts. In Wilson's thought, the problem of reform went beyond throwing the rascals out to ensuring the authority of scientific administrative expertise in a democratic system; the solution was to establish the distinction between administration and politics. Administrative methods could be acquired from any source as long as their application was unbiased—free from partisan politics. Goodnow (1900) made the separation of politics and administration even more explicit: The only thing that would protect the public's will, as expressed by the legislature, from being corrupted in execution was to segregate the two, that is, to limit administrators to carrying out legislative orders in a neutral way.

Early 20th-century reformers in New York and other cities applied the idea of neutral expertise to their reform efforts with considerable enthusiasm. Frederick Cleveland, a leader of the municipal research bureau in New York, declared in his 1909 book that "science is a codification of exactly determined commonsense. . . . The end of science is to establish conclusions that may be accepted without question for purposes of research or instruction" (pp. 176–179). Administration must therefore become a science in order to eliminate confusion and wasteful argument about the best method of accomplishing tasks. In his 1913 work, Cleveland stated that the best thing about America's municipal research bureaus was their "virility" (p. 103). Researchers were not volunteers (a term associated with women) but expert scientists. The municipal researchers' emphasis on scientific expertise led in short order to the founding of a training school in New York to turn out the kind of educated administrators needed in the new scientific approach to municipal government. Although the initial approach was eminently practical, involving trainees in actual projects in city agencies, the idea of a "science of public administration" was not long in coming. Charles Beard, an early director of the training school, envisioned a "new field of public service" with its own distinctive expertise, comprised of administrative law, budgeting and finance, scientific management, public works, personnel, city planning, departmental organization, report preparation, and statistics—a list not too different from today's Master of Public Administration curriculum (Beard, 1916, p. 221).

The separation of administration from politics, with its reliance on scientific objectivity, justified administrative power for more than half a century but fell from grace when the demands of the war effort during the 1940s made it clear that administration and politics were inextricably intertwined—or so goes the conventional wisdom regarding the intellectual history of the field. In actuality, although most observers consider the idea of neutrality out of date, it is still very much with us in the common assumption that in practice expert administrators can rise above their own beliefs and the political fray to fix their sights on the public interest, broadly conceived. But as Harold Seidman has suggested, if the 1937 report of the President's Committee on Administrative Management (the Brownlow Committee) marked the "high noon" of the politics-administration orthodoxy, then someone "apparently stopped the clock" (quoted in Rosenbloom, 1987, p. 78). Like the reform thinkers of a century ago, present-day theorists continue to see public administrators as, at least ideally, objective experts able to perform detached analyses of situations and to weigh claims impartially. For example, Rourke (1992) argues that neutral competence is still the "fundamental element that government bureaucrats bring to the process through which public policy is made . . . and, even more important, that it cannot do without" (p. 539). He calls for reinvigorating professionalism characterized by independent judgment.

These persistent assumptions about the objectivity and neutrality of expertise are fraught with gender contradictions. One of the most enduring patterns in Western thought has been to link the achievement of supposedly unbiased knowledge with masculinity, while tying "Nature," or that which is known, to the female. Francis Bacon conceived of the scientific method as the frank seduction of feminine nature: "I am come in very truth leading to you Nature with all her children to bind her to your service and make her your slave. . . . For you have but to follow and as it were hound nature in her wanderings" (quoted in Keller, 1985, p. 36).[1] The scientific method and its products do not "merely exert a gentle guidance over nature's course; they have the power to conquer and subdue her, to shake her to her foundations. . . . Neither ought a man to make scruple of entering and penetrating into those holes and corners, when the inquisition of truth is its whole object" (quoted in Harding, 1986, p. 116). Whereas nature has been seen as a female to be pursued and forced to yield up her secrets, the seeker after knowledge, at least since Descartes, is a *separated self* who remains detached in order to know and control. Knowledge requires disconnection from the disorderly, feminine field of observation to avoid muddying the results with bias (Bordo, 1987). The cultural masculinity of this mode of knowing, which aims to prevent contamination by removing from the research process all traces of the individual scientist, is implied in the characterization of its products as *hard data*, as distinct from the *soft data* acquired by interactive processes such as interviewing or participant observation. As Keller (1985) argues, the preference for hard over soft data is a reflection of cultural preference for the masculine over the feminine as well as men's historical predominance within science and the societies that science serves.[2]

A number of feminist scholars argue that, because in Western society male children tend to equate self-development and maturity with the attainment of autonomy and separation from their mothers (Chodorow, 1978; Gilligan, 1982), and because men still largely remain in control of social processes, only knowledge gained by means of detachment from the field of observation is seen as qualifying for the term *scientific*—only *this* is really knowledge. According to Keller (1985), this narrow view of the nature of knowledge could only prevail because historically in Western society (white, well-educated) men have set the requirements for knowledge development. Under such circumstances it became possible to universalize a set of norms that conformed to these men's ways of looking at the world. Over time, the entire society came to see the specific as the universal and other ways of knowing as limited if not flawed in comparison.[3]

The idea of neutrality, which serves in political thought as the equivalent of objectivity, is a fundamental tenet of the classical liberalism that undergirds American government. To preserve individual freedom and equality, the liberal state must maintain neutrality with respect to individual preferences; the state serves simply as a referee, managing the process by which claims compete. Yet, as feminist theorists have shown, this claim of neutrality dissolves when one focuses on the extent to which liberal thought—and the state that took shape in tandem with it—depends on women's continued exclusion from the public space where competition among political equals is supposed to take place. As Mary Astell put it in 1700, "If all Men are born free, how is it that all Women are born slaves?" (quoted in Jaggar, 1983, p. 27).

While political theories that rationalized the existence of monarchy had not been inconsistent with the subordination of women (after all, compared to a monarch all subjects are subordinate), the liberal claim of individual freedom based on human rationality made women a problem for political philosophers. Logic dictated either that women, as human beings, were rational and therefore possessed equal liberty with men or that, despite being human, they were somehow deficient in rationality and therefore deserved to be barred from public life. The typical way of overcoming this dilemma was to assert women's equality in theory but defend their continued inequality in practice on instrumental grounds, such as the need to maintain the integrity of home and family. For example, Locke argued that although theoretically women are free to overcome their "natural limitations" their physical weakness justifies practices that subordinate them (see Butler, 1978). Thus, for women today it may be less easy than it is for men to see the liberal idea of government neutrality as unproblematic. The state has never been neutral on the subject of women—in fact, at the time when Wilson and Goodnow were urging administrative neutrality, women still could not vote. If Wilson, who was teaching at Bryn Mawr College when he penned his famous essay in 1887, had listened to his students (all females) on the issue of suffrage instead of disdaining and patronizing them, he might have been more cautious about concluding that "the weightier debates of constitutional principle" were "no longer of more immediate practical moment than questions of administration" (p. 200).[4]

The viability of the idea of objective expertise depends heavily on sustaining confidence in reason's effectiveness as a means of acquiring knowledge. Numerous observers have suggested that the development of the professions during the 19th century involved setting an exaggerated value on reason at the expense of the emotions. Bledstein (1976) notes that the heavy emphasis on rationality during this time stemmed from the anxiety of the middle-class man over the threat of failure to "prove himself tough-minded and vigilant—a man" and about "losing out to the competition and being compromised" (pp. 114–115). Haber's (1964) study of scientific management points out how faith in science introduced standards of disinterestedness and rigor into managerialism, with its interest in guidance and control of organizational processes. Ginzberg (1990) argues that the desire to professionalize social work made it necessary to discount the value of middle-class women's volunteer work on the basis that femininity was essentially irrational: "Increasingly, male values were viewed as necessary to control and limit a female effusion of emotion, sensibility, or passion; either those sensibilities would submit to law and system or they would become entirely ineffective, even dangerous" (p. 173).

Certainly, both men and women of the 19th century saw feminine feeling as a threat to the impartiality of professional judgment, which was (and is) typically thought to depend on the exercise of dispassionate reason. Young (1987) explains that impartiality connotes "being able to see the whole," which means being able to "stand outside and above the situation," a move that can only be made by the separated self (pp. 60–61). The impartial reasoner aims to banish uncertainty and bias by eliminating the specifics of situations; through detachment, which facilitates seeing all possible perspectives, the reasoner need not consult with real people. In addition, being impartial means being *ruled* by reason—in the sense not simply of having reasons but of reducing "objects of thought to a common measure, to universal laws" (p. 61). Such reason entails being unaffected by feelings; "only by expelling desire, affectivity and the body from reason can impartiality achieve its unity" (p. 62). In contrast, decisions based on sympathetic understandings, on caring, are defined as sentimental.

McSwite (1997) has characterized the entire history of public administrative thought as marked by the ideal figure of the Man of Reason. Citizens can rest easy, according to the typical argument, because the Man of Reason is making decisions through submission to objective reality, meaning that which is outside (i.e., the external world), "in which fact and falsehood/good and bad interact to produce an inescapable context, a reality that cannot be avoided and that must be acknowledged and respected" (p. 233). The image of the Man of Reason, although not specifically labeled as such, appears throughout the development of the field—for example, in the "passion for anonymity" that characterized the Brownlow Committee's ideal administrator, which appears to promise the impersonality necessary to justify administrative power by keeping it uncontaminated by politics. But as a practical matter, such anonymity becomes more difficult to sustain when administrators themselves become a diverse group. Administrators can only be counted on to maintain a posture of anonymity, of objectivity, if their individual identities have no effect on their actions. One can only have a passion for anonymity if one is willing and able to identify—at least in practice if not in one's heart—with accepted agency viewpoints and methods, a move that is problematic for people who have, until relatively recently, been restricted to the margins of bureaucracy, if not barred from it entirely. As women and people of color infiltrate decision-making processes in public organizations, the assumption that everyone in the agency holds the same norms in common becomes less dependable. In recognition of this, theories of "representative bureaucracy" (e.g., Krislov, 1974), which stress the hiring of personnel who reflect the demographics of their jurisdictions, not only assume that people's viewpoints are affected by their race, class, and gender but actually treat such linkages as an asset in achieving bureaucratic responsiveness.

One might protest that no one in public administration any longer advocates a passion for anonymity. But scholars continue to justify administrative discretion on the basis that it represents the agency perspective rather than that of any one individual. The best-known argument is that of Wamsley and his colleagues (1990): They have advocated recognizing agencies as "repositories of . . . specialized knowledge, historical experience, time-tested wisdom, and most importantly, some degree of consensus as to the public interest relevant to a particular societal function" (p. 37). And so agencies undoubtedly are—but surely the point of the agency perspective is that, by buying into it, an individual administrator takes on the identity of the agency and in so doing reduces the risk of idiosyncrasy in decision making. The individual becomes anonymous in the sense of serving as a reliable surrogate for the agency as a whole. It would seem, however, that a coherent agency perspective, particularly one with a historical dimension, would have to have been shaped by the identities of the persons who have comprised the agency over time. An agency with a mostly white middle-class male professional membership will find it easier to reach the common perspective to which the Blacksburg theorists look than could be the case once the agency membership becomes more diverse. The Blacksburg argument, despite its attempt to take situational factors seriously, falls into the same conceptual trap as the Brownlow passion for anonymity; that is, it fails to consider both the partiality of a perspective developed by a narrow range of humanity and the impact of increasing public work force diversity on the continuing achievement of a shared point of view. I do not mean to suggest that a common frame of reference is impossible or that it might not be desirable. I do argue that the detachment from the body and from life experience required by a norm of objectivity, by the image of the Man of Reason, leads theorists to overestimate the universality of certain values and approaches and the ease of developing a shared perspective. We will not attain a truly contextual understanding of public administrative practice until we open up what now passes for the agency perspective to the views, values, and perceptions of *others* (nonwhite, non-male) who are increasingly inside agencies where they were once mainly clients of them. If the agency perspective is to serve as a real alternative to administrative anonymity, we must examine the ways in which it is constructed and take into account the transformative potential of placing real, as distinguished from lip service, value on diversity.

Professional Autonomy

> The culture of professionalism incarnated the radical idea of the inde-
> pendent democrat, a liberated person seeking to free the power of
> nature within every worldly sphere; a self-governing individual exer-
> cising his trained judgment in an open society. The Mid-Victorian as
> professional person strove to attain a level of autonomous individual-
> ism, a position of unchallenged authority heretofore unknown in
> American life. (Bledstein, 1976, pp. 87–88)

Bledstein's (1976) study of the development of professionalism during the 19th century places appropriate stress on the notion of autonomy. Most treatments of professionalism in the sociological literature center on control over the content and conditions of work as a defining feature (e.g., Vollmer & Mills, 1966). Professional knowledge and its applica-tion in practice are said to be so specialized that no outsider is qualified to judge the competence of an individual practitioner or the profession as a whole. Professionals reserve the right to assess what work they are qualified to do as well as the right to police themselves. These rights are so central that groups of workers that reflect other definitive character-istics of professionalism (such as specialized knowledge or a commitment to service) but that lack autonomy in practice have been called *semipro-fessions* in the literature (Etzioni, 1969). In the present context, perhaps it is worth noting that the usual examples given in discussions of semi-professions—social workers, nurses, and other so-called allied health personnel—are predominantly female occupations; this suggests that the ability to make an effective claim of professional autonomy is not unaf-fected by the gender of the groups in question.

As Mosher's (1968) classic discussion argued, the celebrated auton-omy of the professional conflicts with the public administrator's obligation to be responsive to the public interest and to account for his or her actions to elected and politically appointed officials. Yet despite Mosher's sugges-tions, many of the current images of the public administrator continue to imply a high level of autonomy in practice. Rohr (1986) sees public admin-istration as a balance wheel in the system of separated powers, weighing and choosing which of several masters (executive, legislative, or judicial) to obey in particular circumstances. O'Leary and Wise (1991) argue that administrators may choose to cooperate with or resist particular court decisions according to their sense of whether executive branch prerogatives are being encroached on. As a group, public administration theorists worry more about instilling proper values in the hearts of administrators so that their power will be exercised wisely than about imposing limits on their autonomy.[5] Factors that act as limits on the autonomous exercise of administrative discretion, such as civil service regulations, requirements for citizen participation, or due process rules, are typically treated as impediments to administrative effectiveness—as red tape (e.g., Wilson, 1989).

The concern for effectiveness that animates arguments in favor of autonomy in the exercise of administrative discretion is of long standing. White's (1948) observation that the Federalists "had a deep fear of governmental impotence" makes the point in a manner that hints at its underlying masculinity (p. 510). Alexander Hamilton in particular strove to ensure that the federal chief executive would have enough power both to check the irrationality of the legislature and to be proactive and efficacious in the development and implementation of policy. Hamilton's concern for "energy" in the executive branch persists today in the administrator's assertion of the right to autonomy.

In recent literature, this claim has sometimes taken the form of seeing the public administrator as agent of the people or of the public interest. Kass (1990) argues that in law the idea of agency grew out of the need to reduce the isolation that a political economy made up of unfettered individuals can produce, by conceiving of a way for them to act in one another's stead. The agent can work on behalf of others and still retain considerable personal and moral autonomy. Kass notes that "in earliest times, those who acted for others were normally family dependents or bound servants who, in a real sense, were mere extensions of a *pater familias*" (p. 115). Thus the idea of agent evolved in a direction that divested it (whether consciously or not) of the implicit powerlessness associated with women (*family dependents*) or lower-class people (*bound servants*). Wamsley's (1990) image of agency, while it reflects a similar emphasis on acting for others, emphasizes the agent's exertion of responsible power. Wamsley recognizes the tension inherent in two interpretations of agency: one in which the principal acts through the agent (equivalent to Kass's extension of the *pater familias*), the other in which the agent acts on behalf of the principal but not under specific orders. Although either agent could potentially achieve effectiveness, only the latter has autonomy. For Wamsley, the public organization's need for purposive rationality tips the balance in favor of the agential administrator who has autonomy (is, in fact, a *helmsman*), yet he recognizes that the helmsman must still be subordinate to other institutions of government.

The scholarly struggle to develop an image of public administrative autonomy that entails a level of responsiveness sufficient for a representative government reflects a gender dilemma because of the associations we normally make between subordination and femininity. The struggle to think of a way to embrace responsiveness, obedience to the popular will, and compliance with the legitimate dictates of other branches of government, without simultaneously embracing femininity, reflects the effort to retain the sense of separated selfhood—of agency—that is a central feature of our understanding of masculinity. Masculinity is embodied in the self, the knower, the actor, the subject, while the other, that which is known, that which is acted on, the object—these are feminine (de Beauvoir, 1961). As Young (1987) puts it, "An essential part of the situation of being a woman is that of living the ever present possibility that one will be gazed upon as a mere body, as shape and flesh that presents itself as the potential object of another subject's intentions and manipulations, rather than as a living manifestation of action and intention" (p. 66). The public administrator's self-image is of one who sees—but is also seen. In this respect, ironically, the public administrator is like de Beauvoir's woman: As humans, public administrators are subjects, but they are also objects of the gaze of their various masters (agency heads, the legislature, the courts, the people at large). Like women, public administrators must live this contradiction. The form taken by theories of administrative discretion suggest that assertions of autonomy entail unconscious denial of the femininity that lies beneath the image of the responsive administrator.[6]

The Hierarchy of Expertise

The assertion of autonomy is simultaneously a claim of authority, particularly when made within a political context. A number of writers on the Progressive era have commented on this element in the rise of the professional bureaucrat. For example, Skowronek (1982) suggests that the anti-party "good government" thrust of the new 19th-century professional class aimed to counteract efforts by party politicians to bar "the finest culture and highest intellectual power" from positions of influence (p. 43). Wiebe (1967) calls attention to how middle- and upper-class perceptions of societal complexity, fluidity, and disorder became the grounds for promoting the expert authority of the bureaucrat, an argument well illustrated in Woodrow Wilson's (1887) essay "The Study of Administration." Haber

(1964) argues that the Progressive ideology of efficiency promised social harmony once those who were competent led society and conflicting purposes disappeared under the rule of "facts." The men of the New York Bureau of Municipal Research, who inaugurated professional training for administrators, based their entire approach to reforming municipal government on the power of facts to compel agreement about what to do. William Allen, one of the leaders of the Bureau, said that "knowing becomes evidence when it is able to prove the truth to those who do not know and who do not want to know," a statement the power implications of which should be obvious (Allen, 1913, p. 87).

As Bledstein (1976) notes, "Far more than other types of societies, democratic ones required persuasive symbols of the credibility of authority" (pp. 123–124). Professionals in the 19th and early 20th centuries were able to achieve this credibility based on the prestige afforded them by their advanced education and by appealing to the universality and objectivity of "science." Thus Henry Lawrence Gantt, a leader in the movement to professionalize business management, could regard with disdain the "debating society theory of government." In his view, "true democracy is attained only when men are endowed with authority in proportion to their ability to use it efficiently and their willingness to promote the public good. Such men are natural leaders whom all will follow" (quoted in Haber, 1964, p. 48).

The scientific management movement furthered the idea of authoritative expertise; Frederick Taylor (1911) not only distinguished organizational thinking from doing but elevated the former to a position of clear control. He believed the ordinary workman incapable of understanding the science on which the systematization of work was to be based; therefore, efficiency would be served by putting the professional manager—the thinker—in charge of the organization of work while workmen would fulfill their responsibilities by carrying out the manager's directives.

To a considerable extent, assertions of professional authority used terms that reduced those over whom authority would be exerted to a state of dependence. Frequently, this was accomplished through a rhetoric of crisis, abnormality, and disaster. Thus, according to Bledstein (1976), "the culture of professionalism exploited the weakness of Americans—their fears of violent, sudden, catastrophic, and meaningless forces" (p. 102). In a period when the middle class perceived the world as in danger of turning upside down, professionals reassured them, promising to have the expertise necessary to combat these threats, and thereby encouraging "public attitudes of submission and passivity" (p. 104). Wiebe's (1967) characterization of the Progressive era as a "search for order" makes a similar point. Complexity—urbanization, industrialization, immigration, and labor unrest—evoked widespread anxiety, but particularly among elites, who "reached out for mastery" to "quash all disorder" (pp. 76–77).

One can observe this impulse in the rhetoric of Woodrow Wilson's (1887) essay on the study of administration, which begins with the argument that expert administration is made necessary by complexity. Once, "the functions of government were simple, because life itself was simple." But now, "present complexities of trade and perplexities of commercial speculation . . . perennial discords between master and workman . . . assume . . . ominous proportions" (p. 199). The solution, of course, is the science of administration and a public will that is not "meddlesome." Present-day theorists make similar arguments for the need to facilitate the administrator's exercise of discretion. For example, Long (1981) argues that tendencies of political stalemate and policy drift in the rest of government justify the public administrator's authoritative governance. In a polity of "opposing demands," Wildavsky (1990) wonders, "Can we denigrate hierarchy . . . while still honoring public service? Can there be an effective bureaucracy without respect for authority?" (pp. xvii–xviii).

The professional authority-complexity dualism is deeply gendered (Stivers, 1992b). At least since the beginning of the early modern period, the complexity, mystery, or threat that men saw in nature was associated with women, probably because men perceived them as closer to nature as a result of their childbearing and child-rearing responsibilities. The phenomenon of witchcraft is an example of disorder in nature symbolized as feminine (Merchant, 1980). The image of the masculine head of state controlling the unruly, archetypically feminine masses is a notable feature of Western political thought. For example, Machiavelli's body politic is a woman's body, its head a male head. The true prince renders the people "submissive, grateful, loyal" (Brown, 1988, pp. 87–88, 109–110). John Knox argued that the ruler (head or mind) of the body politic must be a man, for women's rule would be monstrous (Merchant, 1980). From the feminist perspective, the persistence of this dualism represents the heroic masculine ego's projection of the psyche's inner complexity onto the world. The threat to the sense of authority and control must originate in the world and not from within the self. Young (1987) notes that this dichotomy is hierarchical rather than symmetrical: not only are self and world distinct but self assumes primacy over world.

The image of the public administrator as authoritative expert has troubling ramifications for three groups that in practice occupy the subordinated, feminized status of *other*. First, the expert administrator's translation of the life experiences and political claims of *clients* into depoliticized needs that can be handled bureaucratically turns clients from intentional agents capable of dealing with their predicaments meaningfully, if not unaided, into passive recipients of government services (Fraser, 1990). From the administrative perspective, the best client is one who follows advice, has no problems that do not fit the regulations, and is grateful for benefits received; in other words, the desirable client, regardless of sex, has culturally feminine characteristics. Second, the hierarchical character of professionalism blocks the potential for genuine dialogue with *citizens*, whose opinions can more easily be discounted or dismissed because they are not considered expert. For the administrator, the best citizen is one who is decorative rather than substantive and who understands the citizen role as follower, supporter, and ratifier rather than as co-equal. Finally, professionalism's equation of merit with advanced education blocks the mobility of nonprofessional *workers* in the bureaucracy, who are disproportionately women and people of color (Allen, 1987), and by inhibiting perceptions of mutual interest hinders the formation of alliances among professional and nonprofessional women (Franzway et al., 1989). Thus the authority of professional expertise feminizes clients, citizens, and other workers—and I hope it is clear by now that feminization refers to a political rather than a biological condition.

Lane and Wolf's (1990) reference to secretarial workers (rare in the literature) reflects the implicit acceptance of professional authority in the way it ignores the gender dimensions of this observation:

> The clerical and administrative support staffs play an undervalued but essential role in the effective maintenance of the administrative processes of government. . . . It is this clerical staff that can be relied upon to know which person to call and what pitfall to avoid . . . [and] is often the most reliable and complete repository for [agency] strengths, foibles, and sensitivities. . . . Unfortunately, these capacities are often tied to lower-status occupational positions, so their importance is overlooked and performance poorly rewarded. (p. 69)

In the process of chastising others for overlooking the importance of clerical workers, Lane and Wolf have evidently overlooked the fact that the secretarial staff is made up almost entirely of females—or, if they have noticed it, they evidently attach no significance to it. They deserve credit for pointing out the contribution that low-status and low-authority employees make to agency effectiveness; but without specific attention to gender, and the role it plays in keeping disproportionate numbers of female public employees in these ill-paid, low-power positions, the observation has a patronizing ring.

Brotherhood

In a 1915 presentation to the precursor of the National Association of Social Workers, Abraham Flexner (whose report on medical education speeded the professionalization of the physician) commented, "A profession is a brotherhood. . . . Professional activities are so definite, so absorbing in interest, so rich in duties and responsibilities, that they completely engage their votaries. The social and personal lives of professional men and their families thus tend to organize around a professional nucleus" (quoted in Glazer & Slater, 1987, p. 175). Flexner's observation highlights an aspect of professionalism that has been little noted in the literature of public administration: that it is a subculture, a community, an association. Banding together in formal association originally meant to professionals the ability to set agreed-upon standards of competence and codes of conduct, so as to protect the public (Lubove, 1965). But as every student of Selznick (1957) knows, the institutionalization of a social phenomenon like professionalism is not a neutral process of formal organization but entails the establishment of values. As they come together, members of a profession take on a shared set of norms and a way of seeing the world in common. This professional culture sets them apart from the rest of society. Wiebe (1967) notes, "Identification by way of skills gave [Progressive era professionals] the deference of their neighbors. . . . The shared mysteries of a specialty allowed intimate communion even at long range" (p. 113).

The professional emphasis on like-mindedness runs the risk of expanding into exclusivity based on ascriptive characteristics rather than on learning. Historically, restricting entrance to people of similar race, gender, and class appeared to strengthen bonds of trust among members of professions and assured them that ideas could be shared easily in a style with which they all identified. Although the professions have lifted formal restrictions based on race and gender, patterns of membership established under these rules have been slow in dissipating—even today, for instance, the continued existence of medical and dental societies oriented to African-American professionals suggests that people of color do not perceive the mainstream societies as sufficiently hospitable to them. At any rate, professionals have a perennial tendency to promote their unique perspective, mystifying their subject matter to veil the intuition and guesswork that inevitably supplement scientific judgment; exclusivity helps ensure that those who are uninitiated in the uncertainties of practice remain that way—that the "fabric of legitimacy" endures (Glazer & Slater, 1987, pp. 238–239).

But there is more to professional brotherhood than simply its resistance to diversity. As Flexner noted, professional work is expected to be all-absorbing; therefore, it requires a family willing to organize itself around the requirements of professional work and to provide the necessities of life that single-minded devotion to career leaves the professional no time to worry about. Laws (1976) calls this

> the myth of the heroic male professional . . . a model of work motivation which is used as the standard for assessing all other workers. . . . His work is the most important thing in his life. . . . [His] career is so demanding as to preclude other major commitments. . . . The heroic male professional sacrifices "selfish" concerns like personal and family life to the demands of his career. (p. 36)

Because the heroic male professional is an ideal type or image that sets the standard for performance, workers who refuse or cannot afford to "sacrifice selfish family concerns" are perceived to be less accomplished, less committed, less worthy of advancement. Because women still bear a disproportionate amount of responsibility for family life and because most are still socialized to believe that family needs come before career success, they make up most of these "lesser" workers. Women who try to pursue a dual career of professional and domestic work find themselves pretending that they are single-mindedly focused on the office and that their children's problems never intrude on their organizational lives. When they indicate their inability to work evenings and weekends, bosses gradually come to perceive them as less dedicated or less hardworking than their male colleagues, and as a result they are passed over at promotion time.

Thus the term brotherhood is apt: Professional membership is problematic for women in a way that it is not for men. To be professionals, women must figure out how to close the gap between themselves and the perceived norms of membership—images of how a "real" member looks and acts; they must also deal with much greater difficulty attaining the level of devotion to work expected of members. In the current professional subculture, women are apt, no matter how much they struggle to learn the lingo, to continue to feel like aliens.

Professionalism and Women

As a way of summarizing and reflecting back on the images of the public administrator as expert, let us consider the challenges faced by the female bureaucrat who aspires to the status of professional expert. As should be clear by now, my argument is that defending the power of public administrators on the basis of their competence is problematic because the resulting image of the public administrator (a) privileges masculine characteristics while denigrating and/or suppressing feminine ones and (b) depends for its coherence on maintaining women in a position of inequality with respect to life chances and resources. There may be a way of thinking about administrative competence that does not entail seeing traditionally feminine qualities as inferior and keeping women at a disadvantage; if there is, the problem is not using expertise per se as a basis for defending the legitimacy of public administration but, rather, the notion of expertise we use. To understand the difficulty fully, let us consider the impact on women in public administration on the questions raised above.

In general, the effect on women is one of dissonance between the status woman and the status professional expert. Professional administrators are expected to (a) be technically expert, objective, and impartial; (b) merge without difficulty into their agency's perspective; (c) display autonomous authority in the exercise of discretion; (d) share a worldview and set of values with like-minded fellow members of the profession; and (e) regard their work as primary in their lives—to devote long hours and uninterrupted years to it and to put its demands ahead of personal concerns. Societal expectations of women are, in almost every respect, polar opposites. Women are expected to be good at sensing other people's feelings, at caring about them and nurturing them; in the agency setting (as we saw in Chapter 2) they are perceived as different, even problematic; although hope of their continued submissiveness has dimmed, they are still expected to be responsive to men and in their heart of hearts to prefer marriage to a head of household over independence and autonomy; they are still widely seen as not authoritative and ill-suited to the exercise of authority; their values are perceived not only as different from men's but less worthy (Gilligan, 1982)—thus the extent of their professional like-mindedness is in question; and they are expected to put home and family ahead of (or at least equal to) career and to bear the brunt of household responsibilities.

Thus women who pursue careers as professional public administrators are faced with a dilemma—the fundamental inconsistency between what is expected of them as women and what is expected of them as professional experts. As we have seen, it is not just that professional characteristics are culturally masculine but that in addition they give masculinity an advantage over femininity and depend on structural arrangements that make it difficult for women to meet professional expectations. Thus it is fraudulent to offer women an equal opportunity to pursue a public service career and rise through the ranks of the bureaucracy while at the same time the requirements and exemplary qualities for that sort of career remain incongruent with what is expected of them as women.

To observe that a number of women have done it successfully is to miss the point. They have virtually never done it without a constant effort to manage their femaleness on the job (tackling issues such as how to appear authoritative yet not masculine) and without a continuing struggle to balance work and home responsibilities. Many men may also feel some distance between their sense of self and what the image of the professional expert requires, but they never have to choose between being experts and being seen as masculine, and rarely do they assume a level of household duties, routinely borne by women, that significantly interferes with job requirements. When they do, like women their careers suffer because their attitudes are seen as insufficiently professional.

Thus the arguments for competence as a basis for the legitimacy of public administration entail a logic and a set of societal arrangements in which women and women's qualities are at a disadvantage. In concluding this discussion, I want to emphasize that it is not only women but the profession as a whole that struggles with a paradox that has gender dimensions. I mentioned earlier that public administration's stress on autonomy, on not simply taking orders but instead making discretionary decisions, is a culturally masculine concern in tension with the stereotypically feminine obligation to be responsive. One could argue that other aspects of public administration's political role are similarly feminine—for example, the norm of service. At the level of cultural ideology, it is women who serve others while men are served; women unselfishly devote themselves to helping the unfortunate while men pursue self-interest, albeit sometimes the enlightened variety. If what makes public administrators different from other experts is their responsibilities of service and responsiveness, then as a group they too, like women, do not fit the professional role very well. Professionalism is too masculine for the feminine aspects of public administration. In this context, the effort to assert the worth of public administration in such terms as professional, helmsman, agent, objective scientist, and neutral expert is an effort to acquire masculinity and repress femininity or project it outward. In this sense, public administration is not only masculinist and patriarchal, it is in fundamental denial as to its own nature and conceptually and practically impoverished as a result. Women are not the only ones in public administration faced with a gender dilemma. Theorists may extol the virtues of the responsive, caring bureaucrat who serves the public interest, but the argument will face uphill sledding until we recognize that responsiveness, caring, and service are culturally feminine qualities and that, in public administration, we are ambivalent about them for that very reason.

Notes

1. According to Adams (personal communication, 1991), Bacon asserted that we must put nature "to the rack to compel her to answer our questions." Similarly, Galileo spoke of a need in our investigations of nature to "commit a rape of the senses."

2. Harding (1986) notes that feminist criticism of the detached, masculine self bears striking resemblance to Africanist criticism of the individualistic European self.

3. For a more in-depth discussion of these views as they apply to public administration, see Stivers (1992b).

4. In Wilson's October 20, 1887, entry in his diary, he complained, "Lecturing to young women of the present generation on the history and principles of politics is about as appropriate and profitable as would be lecturing to stone masons on the evolution of fashion in dress" (quoted in Blagdon, 1967, p. 143). Blagdon (1967) comments that Wilson did not believe in higher education for women. Wilson continued to oppose female suffrage until 1918, when militant suffragists embarrassed him by picketing the White House carrying placards with quotations from his League of Nations speeches, such as "Liberty for the world but none at home."

5. In terms of the classic debate between Carl Friedrich (1940) and Herman Finer (1940) on this issue, Friedrich's position, that the ultimate rein on administrative power is the administrator's inner sense of responsibility to the profession as well as to public opinion, has been in the ascendancy for some time over Finer's insistence on concrete external checks—perhaps ever since the debate itself. McSwite (1997) notes that, despite their differences, Friedrich and Finer are united in subscribing to the idea that a conscious, rational attitude is essential to effective action.

6. In a similar but class-based analysis, Derber (1983) suggests that salaried professionals forfeit the right to make decisions about work objectives while exacting from employers compensatory privileges like status and technical autonomy; thus their expertise is put to the service of goals they do not choose. Derber argues that the reluctance of bureaucratic professionals to examine the extent to which agency goals diverge from their own interests and values reflects an unconscious denial of the extent to which they have been proletarianized.

4

"Look Like a Lady, Act Like a Man"
The Dilemma of Leadership

Theorists frequently justify the exercise of administrative power on the basis that it fills a need for public leadership. The rationale is based on the nature of the American system of government and politics. Both scholars and practitioners tend to see this system as characterized by complexity, turbulence, and fragmented power, all of which hinder governance. The argument runs as follows: A federal system marked by separation of powers and checks and balances and a politics driven by the conflicting demands of competing interest groups not only keep power from coalescing but also make it difficult to govern. Under such conditions, there is a great need for stability and vision, for people who can see beyond the contention and roadblocks that plague immediate issues, develop strategies and long-range plans, keep things overall on some sort of coherent course, resist the political urge to sacrifice basic capacities for short-term gains, generate new ideas for dealing with persistent social problems—and who have enough authority and power to bring a modicum of order and rationality into the turbulent arena of government. Structurally, the argument concludes, because the career civil service entails continuity, stability, and a broad purview on the overall system, it is the ideal place to look to for this guiding vision.

In Chapter 3, I argued that public administration uses the fragmented nature of American government and politics to justify professional autonomy. Here I suggest that apparent complexity and political uncertainty also serve as warrants for an argument that, as leaders who have the vision necessary to steer the ship of state and as stewards of fundamental administrative capabilities, public administrators play a crucial role in governance and therefore merit the respect of other governmental actors and the general public.

This approach to justifying administrative discretion sees it not as a professional function but as an organizational phenomenon, a form of management. This is especially the case over the past decade or so, when the idea of "the public manager as leader" spread as the so-called public management school of thought gained strength. Members of this school distinguish the notion of public management from what they refer to as "traditional public administration," a term meant to connote theoretical emphasis on bureaucratic routines and regulations in conceptualizing administrative practice. Rejecting a long-standing distinction between management and leadership in which managers primarily control organizational processes whereas leaders at the top set the mission and vision, members of the public management school argue that, as Behn (1998) puts it, "leadership from public managers is needed because without leadership public organizations will never mobilize themselves to accomplish their mandated purposes, let alone figure out how best to do that" (p. 209).

As Behn's position implies, the organizational perspective in public administration emphasizes success in attaining agency goals. For example, Doig and Hargrove's (1987) study of public sector leaders argues that "because fragmentation and decentralization create checks and balances that obstruct 'orderly' innovation . . . there will be a need for talented men and women who can define new goals, build coalitions that knit together public and private interests, and carry out other entrepreneurial tasks required in this society of great diversity" (pp. 19–20). Exemplary administrative leaders, by means of vision, drive, and ambition, make their mark on agencies and society at large as they develop and husband organizational capacities. Doig (1988), drawing on the work of Joseph Schumpeter, describes this sort of leader as an entrepreneur: someone who is rational and egotistical, who has the "will to found a private kingdom . . . the impulse to fight, to prove oneself superior" and who is motivated by the "joy of creating, of getting things done, or simply of exercising one's energy and ingenuity" (p. 21). The "reinventing government" movement (Osborne & Gaebler, 1992), which has become a veritable civic religion in American governments at all levels, characterizes the entrepreneurial spirit as a transformative force in the public sector:

> It is willing to abandon old programs and methods. It is innovative and imaginative and creative. It takes risks. It turns city functions into money makers rather than budget busters. It eschews traditional alternatives that offer only life support systems. It works with the private sector. It employs solid business sense. It privatizes. It creates enterprises and revenue generating operations. It is market oriented. It focuses on performance measurement. It rewards merit. It says "Let's make this work," and it is unafraid to dream the great dream. (p. 18)

To be sure, there are theorists who are critical of the image of the public administrator as entrepreneurial manager/leader, but they have their own arguments for the importance of leadership. Terry (1990), for example, is critical of the entrepreneurial model but views the desired leader as a conservator, that is, someone who is necessary to preserve the "institutional integrity" of public organizations and to maintain the organization's "distinctive competence" (p. 404). Cook (1998) argues that public administrators exercise leadership by "fulfilling, maintaining, and enhancing the character of the regime" (p. 228). Keller (1988) criticizes what he sees as overemphasis in the literature on goal accomplishment, particularly what he sees as decided stress on "skillful manipulation and buffering," but he, too, ends by calling for effective constitutional manager-leaders (pp. 71–72).

Mitchell and Scott (1987) suggest that arguments justifying public administration based on the need for public sector leadership are quite powerful when linked, as they usually are (at least implicitly), to the notion of professional expertise. Couched in terms that draw heavily on organization theory developed largely in the context of private business, the leadership argument suggests that only a few have the skill and vision to lead and that these few dwell, as administrators, in interdependent public and private organizations. More important, administrators have the right to draw economic benefits from their organizations without suspicion of economic exploitation. They are receiving their just deserts for doing a job few could do (p. 447).

The questions these arguments raise for the place of women in public administration have to do with the intellectual baggage and material circumstances that, though we are usually unaware of them, support images of leadership and thus shape our understanding. For example, we might first want to ask why the idea of leadership has a legitimating effect despite there being little unarguable evidence that the variable *leadership* actually has a clear impact on situations where it is thought to be important:

> Decades of academic analysis have given us more than 350 definitions of leadership. Literally thousands of empirical investigations of leaders have been conducted in the last seventy-five years alone, but no clear unequivocal understanding exists as to what distinguishes leaders from non-leaders. . . . Never have so many labored so long to say so little. (Bennis & Nanus, 1985, p. 4)

After all this research, the most we seem able to say is that leadership is partly a matter of personal qualities and partly contingent on the situation. Yet books, articles, and conference presentations continue to call for "better leadership" as the answer to the problems of public agencies.

Leadership has become public administration's *phlogiston*—the mysterious substance that, prior to the discovery of oxygen, was believed to be the ingredient in substances that made them burn. Our continued reliance on such a vague concept suggests that its function is ideological, in two senses of the word. Leadership is an important cultural myth by which we make sense of and impart significance to organizational and political significance; in addition, leadership is an idea used to support and rationalize the continuation of existing political, economic, racial, and gender arrangements.

In what follows, I approach leadership as an image that functions in the context of public agencies to maintain existing patterns of discrimination against women, particularly against women of color and working-class women. Images of organizational leadership in Western industrialized societies have been developed in situations dominated by white, professional men and therefore not surprisingly reflect the personal characteristics, worldviews, and values of those who historically have occupied leadership positions. The result is that those who are not white, male, or professional tend to fit—or more accurately, tend to be perceived as fitting—the leadership image rather poorly. People who fail to qualify on two or three of these counts (for example, a female of color who occupies a support staff position) are likely to have more difficulty moving into and occupying leadership status than those who fail to measure up on only one count (Travis, 1991).

My consideration of the image of leadership begins by summarizing, based on the literature in public administration and business management, what leadership appears to mean to us in organizational life. The discussion critiques five images of leadership:

1. The leader as visionary, one who has the enlarged understanding and insight necessary to guide public organizations

2. The leader as decision maker, one who can take charge and move the organization forward

3. The leader as manager, a planner and strategizer who exerts control over organizational elements, including personnel, in order to reach defined goals

4. The leader as symbol, one who influences and motivates followers

5. The leader as definer of reality, one who tells or shows others the meaning of their work.

I then review ideas about women leaders, both sexist stereotypes and the views of those who argue that because of their life experiences and values women tend to practice a more interactive, nurturant form of leadership than the mainstream one. Next, I deal with women's leadership dilemma, that is, the fundamental conflict that exists between, on one hand, the leadership role and its organizational function, and on the other, feminine gender. I argue that the disparity between images of leadership and norms of femininity force women to struggle to reconcile conflicting demands—"look like a lady" but "act like a man"—a struggle that men, whatever their personal views on leadership, are able to avoid. From this perspective, the optimism of the literature on the strengths and advantages of women's "different" leadership style—the view that as women become leaders they will change organizations— must be at least questioned. The chapter concludes with a few reflections on what this argument implies about the appropriateness of trying to defend public administration on the basis of its ability to provide public leadership.

A Portrait of the Leader

There are three important characteristics that may be crucial to successful innovative action carried out in the complex environment of the government office: a capacity to engage in systematic rational analysis;

an ability to see new possibilities offered by the evolving historical situation; and a desire to "make a difference"—to throw one's energies and personal reputation into the fray in order to bring about changes. (Doig & Hargrove, 1987, p. 11)

A successful organization, it has been said, requires three kinds of individuals: a dreamer, a businessman, and a son-of-a-bitch. In today's leaders, these disparate qualities are merged. (Potts & Behr, 1987, p. 201)

"A man is not a man without a plan." (line by Big Caprice in the movie *Dick Tracy*; quoted in Kerfoot & Knights, 1996, p. 82)

As these quotations indicate, most discussions of leadership include a list of the leader's key qualities, and most feature the leader's vision, decision-making or take-charge capacities, ability to accomplish strategies, and motivational and inspirational ability. Some also argue that we use leaders to help us find significance in what we do—literally, to tell us what our work means.

Let us begin our portrait of the organizational leader by considering the idea of vision. This theme runs through the public administration and business management literatures. Doig and Hargrove (1987) mention "an ability to see new possibilities." Bellavita (1986) suggests that leadership is "an organizational process made up of . . . a vision, . . . political support for the vision; people willing to work to achieve the vision; and the technical ability to carry out the vision" (p. 13). Kotter (1990) tells us that "the direction-setting aspect of leadership does not produce plans; it creates vision and strategies" (p. 104). Potts and Behr (1987) say that "today's more competitive world" requires a leader "who also has the vision to understand what is changing . . . and can adapt quickly to take advantage of that change" (p. 10). Tichy and Ulrich (1984) maintain that the "transformational" leader is one who can develop and communicate a vision and get others to commit to it" (p. 251).

It appears that the leader's vision provides guidance to the organization—helps it find new directions and chart a successful course in a world beset with complexity. In this respect, contemporary organizational literature simply expands on the ideas of classic writers like Barnard and Selznick. Barnard (1948) argued a half century ago that "the primary efforts of leaders need to be directed to the maintenance and guidance of organizations as whole systems of activities," a capacity that in turn requires the ability to distinguish "effectively between the important and the unimportant in the particular concrete situation" (pp. 89, 86). Selznick (1957), for his part, says that the leader "provides guidance to minimize [organizational] blindness . . . his imagination is stirred by the processes of group interaction and the vision of a harmonious team" (pp. 135, 137).

This emphasis on vision as a characteristic leadership quality is notable, say Keller and Grontkowski (1983), because of the centuries-old association between vision and the kind of cognition typically seen as masculine. In ancient Greece, the transition from an oral to a literate culture—from Homer to Plato—produced a change in the idea of knowledge, from identification and engagement with the concrete to detachment and abstraction. The essence of the change is symbolized by a shift in the site of knowledge acquisition from the ear to the eye. In Plato's work, intellect becomes the "eye of the mind" (p. 210); because of its "apparent incorporeality," vision "promotes the illusion of disengagement and objectification" (p. 213). And while for Plato the idea of knowledge included connection with the truth as well as distance from the world, by the time of Newton the eye had become "the means of establishing a total and radical severance of subject and object" (p. 216). Drawing on the work of Hans Jonas, Keller and Grontkowski suggest that vision persists as a metaphor for knowledge because, of all the senses, it alone offers the illusion of timelessness and thus a basis for objectivity and the hope of eternal truth, which I have already suggested are culturally masculine concerns.

If we extend this reasoning to the connection between vision and leadership, a curious relationship between the leader and other members of the organization (the led) begins to emerge. If the leader is a visionary, then others in the situation become objects of the leader's gaze. Grosz (1990) argues, "Vision performs a distancing function, leaving the looker unimplicated in or uncontaminated by its object. . . . As Sartre recognized, the look is the domain of domination and mastery; it provides access to its object without necessarily being in contact with it" (p. 38). Thus vision is not simply a matter of seeing but also of controlling, of fixing and defining those who are the objects of the gaze. I do not mean to imply that these "others" necessarily perceive themselves this way. But if the leader's vision is the required ingredient in organizational coherence, development, and direction, then, without realizing it, other organizational members have ceded control to him not only of the organization but of themselves and crucial aspects of their self-definitions. In the brasher treatments of leadership, this tendency becomes quite explicit, as when Potts and Behr (1987) laud the ability to "see where a company has to go . . . and chart a course that can get the company to that goal, pulling legions of employees along the way" (p. 200).

Consideration of the leader as decision maker reinforces this perception. In public administration, we have thought of the administrator as a decision maker at least since 1887, when Woodrow Wilson in his essay published that year held that "the administrator should have and does have a will of his own in the choice of means for accomplishing his work. He is not and ought not to be a mere passive instrument" (p. 212). Barnard (1948) argued that "the ability to make decisions is the characteristic of leaders I think most to be noted. It depends on a propensity or willingness to decide and a capacity to do so" (p. 94). Today, as Thompson (1985) tells us, "almost all government textbooks refer to political courage as the master virtue in politics, the ability to make decisions" (p. 6). Writers of the public management school emphasize decision making ability as the sine qua non of leadership. As Behn (1998) puts it, "Leaders exercise initiative. . . . They mobilize resources and motivate people. They make choices and explain decisions" (p. 210). Lynn (1996) says that "at the heart of public management . . . is a strategic judgment: a choice concerning goals and actions in specific settings that satisfies reasonable criteria" (p. 91).

The cultural masculinity of the decision maker is revealed in the work of some of our most influential thinkers. For example, Freud argued that people have a need for authority, which, because of its "decisiveness of thought, . . . strength of will . . . [and] energy of action are part of the picture of a father" (quoted in Kets de Vries, 1989, p. 26). According to Bologh (1990), Weber believed strong political leaders would rescue substantive political ends from being overwhelmed by bureaucratic means—in other words, by sheer process. From Weber's perspective, efficiency also required a strong leader; democratizing organizational decision making would undermine rationality. For Weber, "one either adopts a feminine attitude of passivity in which 'life is permitted to run on as an event in nature,' or one adopts a masculine emphasis on decisive action in which life is 'consciously guided by a series of ultimate decisions'" (Bologh, 1990, p. 101).

Feminist organization theorists have also pointed out how decision making and mastery are associated with masculinity. Kanter's (1977) groundbreaking study of gender in organizations argues that men are rewarded for decisiveness, rationality, and visible leadership and women for routine service. In Kanter's view, men and women in effect constitute separate organizational classes regardless of their individual positions in the hierarchy. More recently, Fletcher (1999) suggests that, at least in the case of women professionals (such as engineers) in organizations, the situation is more complex than the notion of "separate classes" conveys. Her research shows that both male and female engineers define "real work" as a kind of "role up the sleeves" decisive problem solving that has the quality of individual heroics. In contrast, the kind of work that results in more effective teams and better communications—in other words, the kind of work for which women have traditionally been said to be suited—"gets disappeared." In fact, it doesn't count as work.

While theorists of public administration invoke gender implicitly rather than explicitly, they reflect a similar emphasis on decisiveness. Terry (1990) praises the proactive efforts of administrative "conservators" to preserve institutional integrity but denounces what he sees as weakness and subservience on the part of public administrators. Rohr's (1989) examination of the "inherent ambiguity" of executive power turns on the tension between the origin of the word executive, which means "follower, or one who carries out" (that is, a clerk) and a more edifying connotation, such as is reflected in the president's executive privilege, in terms of which the executive is "clearly a leader" (p. 108).

Books and articles aimed at private business organizations tend to define leadership by distinguishing it from management. The most cited reference along these lines is John Kotter's (1990) article "What Leaders Really Do." Kotter argues that both managers and leaders decide what needs to be done, create networks of people to accomplish an agenda, then try to make sure the job actually gets done. But managers address these tasks in a different way from that of leaders. Managers concern themselves with ordering the means to get the job done, exercising a list of functions much like the one Luther Gulick (1937) enumerated under the acronym POSDCORB: planning, organizing, staffing, directing, coordinating, reporting, and budgeting. In contrast, leaders set direction, align people, and motivate. The essence of management is control, whereas leaders have a vision, motivate and inspire. The title of Hickman's (1990) book captures the difference as *Mind of a Manager, Soul of a Leader*; Bennis and Nanus (1985) sum it up as follows: "Managers are people who do things right and leaders are people who do the right thing" (p. 21).

Despite these considerable efforts to separate leadership and management, the public management writers insist that managers are and have to be leaders, too. Behn (1998) says that "a public manager takes initiatives publicly. . . . Leaders exercise initiative by articulating and clarifying purposes; by setting and pursuing performance targets; by educating, persuading, and motivating people; by choosing among alternatives; and by experimenting with strategies and tactics" (p. 211). Osborne and Gaebler's (1992) idea of "reinventing government" relies centrally on the idea of managers as entrepreneurial leaders, exercising creative thinking. From the public management perspective, the need for control and stability, a traditional concern of management, has been de-emphasized in favor of freeing managers from what is often referred to as "bureau-pathology," that is, from stifling rules and regulations so that they can take initiative and innovate. Yet the need somehow to bring all this innovation together in a strategic way remains; thus the notion of motivation, a need central to the origin of the very idea of "management," persists.

In the leadership literature, the leader is one who inspires others, who, in Selznick's (1957) words, "knows how to transform a neutral body of men into a committed polity" (p. 61). The leader's inspiration is said to motivate subordinates to carry out their work efficiently (Maccoby, 1988), sometimes to do things beyond their normal capabilities (Kets de Vries, 1989). Even more important, the leader entices workers to put the organization's goals (as defined by its leadership) ahead of their own in return for various inducements (Barnard, 1938). The idea of getting employees to go along with a vision they had no part in devising came out of the late 19th-century struggle between owners and workers "to determine which party would control the technology, training, and personal relationships of the labor process itself" (Jacques 1996, p. 53). Out of this struggle, which owners won with the significant assistance of Frederick Taylor, father of scientific management, came the perceived need for an expert in "handling men": the manager. The word came from the Italian il maneggiare, meaning "one who handles," especially horses. The need for managers came from the recognition that coercion was an insufficient means of control, one that had to be supplemented with persuasion, or "the coordination of the efforts of others [using] the reasoning faculties" (Haines, quoted in Jacques, 1996, p. 129). As Jacques (1996) observes, the concept of motivation implied that technical work rules were not enough to ensure worker compliance.

Concern for motivation came not from entrepreneurs but from corporate engineers, who initiated the "management movement." As conceptualized by engineers, management meant "handling, manipulation. It connotes the specific responsibility for specific results" (Person, 1926, p. 216). In order to ensure desired results, the knowledge and discretion of the worker had to be mobilized. As Jacques (1996) notes, "Of even greater importance [today] are the vast groups of workers who do not need motivation in any traditional sense. Products of disciplinary education and disciplinary society in general, they have internalized a desire to do the job as a means of getting 'ahead' and require of management that it remove barriers rather than induce effort" (p. 160)—as the popularity of reinventing government, one might say, seems to underscore.

Perhaps in recognition of changes in the workforce and lessened need for motivation in the traditional sense, leadership literature emphasizes the leader as an exemplar and symbol of organizational purposes. We hear the corporation referred to as "the lengthened shadow of a man" (Doig & Hargrove, 1987, p. 20), but the shadow also extends beyond organizational boundaries. Lewis (1980) notes that "thousands of would-be public and private managerial types now emulate [leaders] consciously and unconsciously, for [they] have become cultural archetypes" (p. 244). One such archetype might be John F. Welch, Jr., chief executive officer of General Electric:

> They call him Neutron Jack. . . . In the past five years he has cut a swathe through the huge company, overseeing the closing of more than a score of plants and the idling of thousands of workers. When Neutron Jack hits a GE plant town, they, say, the people disappear, but the building stands. . . .
>
> But Welch is no wild-eyed renegade on an ego trip. . . . His overhaul of GE is bringing [it] up to date . . . making . . . GE competitive and successful in [a] rapidly changing world. (Potts & Behr, 1987, pp. 1–3)

Or the exemplar might be Admiral Arleigh Burke: "'30-knot Burke,' the sailors called him . . . because he always kept his task force moving at flank speed. 'This is a guy that sailors would walk off the edge of a cliff for,' [Ross] Perot says. 'He was not a remote, distant figure. He was a guy down there'" (Potts & Behr, 1987, p. 207).

Warrior or father figure, such characters are said to serve as inspirational symbols, spurring the rest of us to extraordinary effort, albeit frequently in aid of goals we have had little part in selecting. That our ability to identify with such figures may vary depending on our own self-images is only imperfectly noted.

The American government's felt need for inspirational leaders is apparently of long standing. As Skowronek (1982) notes, "Federalists and Jeffersonians alike hoped for a consensus of enlightened leaders in a government designed to produce conflicts of interest. . . . Their successes were precariously dependent on the exceptional man [and] the personal loyalties he could instill in others" (p. 24). Crenson (1975) comments that the Jacksonians inherited this dependence, which they reflected in the informal control that executive officers had over their departments: "The personal characteristics and preferences of administrative chieftains carried more weight than formal administrative arrangements" (p. 52). In the Progressive era, Croly (1909/1963) praised the inspirational qualities of Theodore Roosevelt, who "exhibited his genuinely national spirit in nothing so clearly as in his endeavor to give to men of special ability, training, and eminence a better opportunity to serve the public" (p. 170).

Through inspiring organizational members and instilling in them loyalty to the organization and its goals, the leader also shapes their perceptions of the meaning of their work and their lives; in addition to imparting value to rationalized work, the leadership activity that Selznick (1957) called institutionalization is also a process of reality creation. Writers on leadership argue that, through vision, through ability to sense the terms of the organization's environment, and to articulate the organizational mission, the leader "brings order out of chaos. . . . We need someone to look up to or blame. The mere presence of individuals willing to take on the leadership role facilitates the organization of experience and in so doing helps us acquire a sense of control over our environment" (Kets de Vries, 1989, pp. 22-23).

As we saw in Chapter 3, bringing order out of chaos is a culturally masculine idea. The sort of symbolic power in question, of course, extends outside the organization. Crenson (1975), for instance, observes that the emotional bond that Andrew Jackson established between himself and Americans of the time "told men how they felt" (p. 29). In his study of public entrepreneurs, Lewis (1980) notes that J. Edgar Hoover "controlled and specified the reality premises about crime for the whole society" (p. 119). The ultimate power of the leader, then, is in these lines by Alexander Pope: "To make mankind in conscious virtue bold, / Live o'er each scene and be what they behold" (quoted in Wills, 1984, p. 125). If so, then the quality of the symbolic images leaders project is significant for public life as a whole.

Just prior to his inauguration, a *New York Times Magazine* profile on George W. Bush characterized him as "the M.B.A. president." The Bush "dynasty" was described as based in "superior management," that is, management by a member of the Bush family, who all believe that "good management [as evidenced in hiring the right people] makes good politics." About-to-be President Bush commented, "A good executive is one that understands how to recruit people and how to delegate . . . how to align authority and responsibility, how to hold people accountable for results and how to build a team of people" (Bennett, 2001, p. 26). A simultaneous profile of Vice-President-elect Dick Cheney describes him as "CEO of USA Inc.," with President Bush as chairman of the board and Cheney as chief executive. "He is very much a chain of command kind of guy," one aide is quoted as saying. In the corporate world, according to one observer, "[Cheney] was all business . . . nothing touchy-feely. And he immediately asserted his dominance in symbolic ways." The example given of Cheney's approach: "He spent two months studying the management of Halliburton . . . then fired three or four of the top 10" (Milbank, 2001, pp. 6–7). If the leadership literature has anything to say about symbolism, these accounts of President Bush and Vice-President Cheney should send the American people strong signals. The extent to which citizens are ready to emulate, let alone admire, the public leader as businessman remains an open question as the impact of symbolic leadership always does. How much of ourselves must we set aside in the process of rethinking public administration as a business? How white, male, and upper-class are these images, and if they are, how much does this matter for nonwhite, non-male, non-upper-class members of American society? Certainly, while it is not impossible for "different" others to be inspired by upper-class white male leaders, the process is a more complex one than for those who more closely match the image of the typical mainstream leader.

Women Leaders

The characteristics that they criticize you for, that you are strong-minded, that you make firm and tough decisions, are also characteristics which, if you were a man, they would praise you for. I think they have not yet fully come to terms with that.

—Margaret Thatcher
(quoted in "'Iron Lady' Attacks," 1990, p. A1)

Women who move into leadership positions in public agencies find themselves presented with a dilemma. The accepted understanding of leadership entails an image that most white, professional-managerial men fit rather well and others have difficulty matching. In Western industrialized societies, both men and women expect leaders to be decisive, visionary, bold, strategic, and inspirational; as we will see, they also tend to expect leaders to be male. The qualities frequently associated with women, such as intuition and nurturance, are beginning to make their way into discussions of leadership but are still nowhere near being seen as definitive (Stivers, 1991).

As a result, women who become or aspire to become leaders in public agencies are faced with a complex task of self-definition. If they strive to display the expected characteristics, they risk being seen as masculine (inappropriately so, of course) and depending on their individual personalities may feel a certain amount of dissonance between their sense of themselves as women and what is expected of them as leaders. If, on the other hand, they attempt to embody and reflect a different image of leadership than the conventional one, they risk being viewed as unequal to the leadership role—as indecisive, soft, and not assertive enough. "You have to project an image that is feminine enough that you won't be called a dyke," reports a former female captain in the air defense artillery who was investigated and "cleared" of the charge of being a lesbian, "but not so feminine that you won't be taken seriously" (Jamison, 1995, p. 4). Admittedly, some men may also feel a gap between their personal styles and what is expected of leaders, and a man's failure to meet leadership standards is occasionally chalked up to deficient masculinity (for example, the "wimp factor" that plagued George Bush the elder). Men, however, are never criticized as women are for being successful leaders; men are never accused of having undergone the equivalent of a sex change by virtue of having assumed a leadership role.

As a result of this dissonance between womanhood and leadership, a number of stereotypes have grown up about women leaders. The *earth mother* brings cookies to meetings; the *pet* serves as the work group mascot; the *manipulator* uses feminine wiles to get her way; the *workaholic* does not know how to delegate; the *iron maiden* tries too hard and is seen as tyrannical; the *egalitarian* denies her own power by claiming to relate to subordinates as colleagues (Heller, 1982, p. 3). Women leaders who escape such labels often have their images rendered acceptable by more subtle means. For example, Wyszomirski's (1987) portrait of Nancy Hanks describes her in these terms: "A single, attractive, middle-aged woman who combined femininity with a sense of traditional propriety, Hanks became one of only a handful of female federal executives, but she was no feminist" (p. 214). Wyszomirski does not define what she means by "feminist," say why she does not consider Hanks to be one, or specify the basis on which being a feminist is undesirable. Hillary Clinton's experience, however, strongly suggests that it *is* undesirable. Early in her husband's first administration she was described by various critics as a "radical feminist" and "militant feminist lawyer who equates marriage with slavery," a "feminist extremist," a "champion of radical feminism who believes that 12-year-olds should have the right to sue their parents"—charges that led Clinton to soften her appearance and speech (Jamison, 1995, p. 41).

These images convey something of the "damned if you do, damned if you don't" quality of the juggling act in which women leaders engage. Womanhood per se is problematic in the organizational context. Because the stereotypical characteristics of white professional men such as rationality and task orientation match the defining qualities of bureaucracy, we tend to see such qualities (just as we see the organization itself) as neutral rather than masculine. In the bureaucracy, only women have gender and, therefore, a problem accommodating to the dynamics of organizational life. The leader's masculinity is seen as normal, whereas the qualities of the women around him—for example, female secretaries and clients—represent that which the leader is not (helpful, acquiescent); such women are acceptable because they are subordinate and therefore nonthreatening. In contrast, women in nonclerical positions evoke in the male eye (consciously or not) the inappropriate intrusion of the private—the sexual—into the level of public life that men occupy (Hearn & Parkin, 1988). Used to seeing women either as sex objects or as surrogates for their mothers, daughters, or wives, male managers have difficulty seeing them as leaders or peers. Furthermore, as Kanter (1977) argues, the surface similarity between women managers and the largely female clerical staff tends to interfere with women's ability to exercise leadership regardless of their individual management styles or competence.

Research indicates that both men and women overwhelmingly expect leaders to be men, so much so that women in jobs that should logically be considered leadership positions—such as head nurse of a state hospital—have not been generally recognized as such. Wajcman (1996) argues, based on her research, that women who occupy senior positions are indistinguishable in most respects from men in similar positions and that the similarities far outweigh the differences. Nevertheless, she notes, gender stereotypes are still very much alive. For example, 86% of both men and women managers in her study said that men and women were equally good at management. Yet 69% of women and 41% of men said there is a difference in management style based on gender. Both men and women described the male style of management as "directive, self-centered/self-interested, decisive, aggressive, task-oriented," whereas adjectives used to describe the female style included "participative, collaborative, cooperative, coaching style, people-oriented, caring" (p. 342). Interestingly, 81% of both men and women described their own management style as participative; only 19% said they led "from the front, . . . decisively directing subordinates" (p. 343). In other words, as Wajcman notes, "respondents described themselves in terms that fit with the prevailing orthodoxy of good management practice, now strongly associated with a consultative style and a high level of interpersonal skills" (p. 343). But when asked to describe actual behavior in detail, it became clear that women adopted what they otherwise described as a "male" style, what one male manager described as the "Thatcher factor—a tendency to be more stereotypically male than typical male managers" (pp. 345–346). Wacjman argues that the turbulent corporate environment of the 1990s made the actual practice of "soft" management styles seem too risky for managers being held to "hard" performance standards.

Fondas (1997) suggests that a number of popular books on successful management recommend behaviors traditionally considered feminine, such as facilitating, supporting, and nurturing employees. But such behaviors are never labeled "feminine"; rather, writers

struggle openly to find other suitable names or metaphors. As Champy, an expert on reengineering says, "Five years ago [this style] would have been called 'worker democracy.' Three years ago it would have been called 'empowerment'. . . . Whatever it is called it works . . . because he

[i.e., the manager/leader] has built into his redistributed authority
structure a hard-line concern . . . for the quality of the teams' work."
(p. 271)

Fondas observes,

> Notice that managers do not simply have concerns . . . they must have
> a "hard-line" concern, [otherwise] the role might be seen as somehow
> too focused on concern and caring. Indeed, the author later stated that
> he inserted "hard-line" because the managers insisted their behavior
> be seen as "realistic" and "hard," not exclusively people-oriented or
> "soft." (p. 271).

Other research underscores the persistence of gender stereotypes: for
example, Carli and Eagly (1999) found that, in general, people consider
men to be more assertive, daring, and competitive and women to be more
gentle, kind, and supportive. Similarly, men are thought to be more analytical and better at abstractions and problem solving, and women are
seen as more imaginative, verbally skilled, and creative. As the researchers
note, women's skills are not thought to be important to success in task-
oriented groups: "In fact, a double standard exists. What constitutes a
high level of competence is higher for women than for men. This phenomenon means that women must perform better to be considered equally
competent, regardless of whether group members evaluate themselves or
other group members" (p. 211). Astin and Leland (1991) point out that,
while studies show no clear patterns of difference in behavior between
male and female leaders, subordinates react differently to similar behavior
according to whether the leader is a man or a woman. These authors also
note that much of the research on the relationship between gender and
leadership has been conducted in terms of traditional models such as trait
theory, contingency theory, and so on that have been developed largely in
laboratory or other settings where males predominate.

The lopsided organizational distribution of the sexes, with men occupying all but a few of the top positions and women concentrated in
low-level clerical and staff support positions, is a structural source of
expectations about leadership. There are many factors influencing the discriminatory practices that result in this apportionment, including cultural
values that assign men responsibility for public activities and women private ones, and organizational expectations that white-collar men will be
mind workers and white-collar women manual workers. In addition, some

observers theorize the existence of a dual labor market in which women function as a "reserve army of labor" based on their performance of household and child-care duties (Hearn & Parkin, 1988, p. 18); capitalism's structural necessity for surplus workers supports patterns in which women are disproportionately restricted to low-level, often part-time, positions.

The feedback loop between the sexual distribution of labor and people's expectations about who will occupy what job means that women who aspire to leadership roles encounter material and mental barriers to their access to such positions; when they do manage to move into a leadership position, women face the difficult task of managing their femininity. The management literature reflects no small amount of advice on how to do this but little if any acknowledgment that it is anything but an individual problem. One line of thought simply accepts the mainstream definition of leadership and advocates the elimination of barriers to women's access to top positions. This approach is characteristic of liberal feminism, which advocates a piece of the existing action for women. The expectation is that as women become leaders and show that they can be tough, bold, and so on, leadership will gradually lose its association with masculinity. In the leadership literature based on this view, the focus is on teaching women to be better at leadership as men have exemplified it, in order for them to qualify for the equal opportunities that revamped hiring and promotion practices are said to open up to them. Themes include fitting in and learning the men's game. These books tell women they are responsible for their own success or failure in adapting to organizational life; their primary task is to adjust their own femaleness. Harragan's (1981) *Games Mother Never Taught You*, for example, advises women to use football jargon and military imagery around the office. *Leadership Skills for Women* by Manning (1989) counsels "business-like clothing and sensible heels that increase your height. . . . [Use] strong, direct language. . . . Do not overuse hand gestures. . . . Do not flirt. . . . Don't try to be 'one of the boys'" (p. 15).

In recent years, considerable attention has been paid to the possibility that, because, on average, women have different personal qualities and life experiences than men, they tend to approach organizational leadership distinctively and that these differences may benefit organizations, helping them achieve the greater flexibility required in an age of increasing complexity. From this perspective, the task is not to try and wipe out women's feminine qualities but to use them to enhance organizational effectiveness. This argument is characteristic of what is known as "difference feminism" (e.g., Gilligan, 1982). Women's management styles are said to be less hierarchical and more participatory: "Women value connections and community sharing power. We want the world to be a family," says management consultant Bev Forbes (quoted in Grubb, 1991, p. 18). Rosener's (1990) often-cited *Harvard Business Review* article argues that while men use and command-and-control style, women leaders try "to make people feel part of the organization . . . encouraging others to have a say in almost every aspect of the work. . . . They create mechanisms that get people to participate and they use a conversational style that sends signals inviting people to get involved" (p. 120). Helgesen's (1990) case study of four women executives, which examined how they differed from the males studied in Mintzberg's (1973) well-known *The Nature of Managerial Work*, reported that the women departed significantly from Mintzberg's picture of ordinary managerial behavior: They were willing to be interrupted by unscheduled tasks and visits, out of a desire to keep the organizational fabric in good repair; they shared rather than hoarded information; instead of identifying wholly with their careers, they saw themselves as multifaceted. Along similar lines, a *New York Times* profile of Grace Pastiak, director of manufacturing for Tellabs, Inc., described her as preferring a personalized, walking-around approach, trying to imbue her subordinates with the enthusiasm for quality (Holusha, 1991).

The expectation reflected in much of the writing in this vein is that as more women move into leadership positions, organizations themselves will begin to change—will become less hierarchical, more participatory, and more humane. Yet much of the research informing this perspective has been criticized for inadequate techniques. Powell's (1993) review of research on women and men in management concludes that there is little evidence that the two sexes approach leadership and management distinctively. Powell argues that in order to demonstrate a difference we would have to know more about female-dominated organizations. "Do women at the top, who answer to no one, lead differently? . . . In a female organization, do men have to act like women? We don't have enough data" (quoted in Noble, 1993, p. 36). Kanter (1980) also counsels skepticism. She suggests that whatever differences are perceived between men's and women's organizational behavior are a function of power rather than gender: "Every statement that can be made about what women typically do or feel holds true for some men. . . . What appear to be 'sex differences' in work behavior emerge as responses to structural conditions, to one's place in the organization" (p. 57).

Arguments such as these raise two possibilities. One is that feminine management techniques, despite the praise they now seem to be receiving in certain quarters, remain disadvantageous to women overall, and perhaps to men who adopt them as well. They tend to reinforce cultural stereotypes that work against women's access to top jobs and, for both women and men, can trigger suspicions about whether they are tough enough to handle leadership responsibilities. The other possibility, as we have seen, is that attention to women's leadership styles is simply a reflection of a current trend toward participatory management styles; men and women, however, appear to be concluding that, ultimately, "soft" styles are too risky, which suggests that humane management styles may simply be a fad intended to ease the process of getting employees to buy into organizational goals set at the top (Argyris, 1957; Grenier, 1988). In this case, "feminine" leadership is not really in the process of transforming organizations, only of masking their real (hierarchical) nature more effectively. Meanwhile, the feedback loop between the sexual distribution of labor in organizations and people's expectations about who can do which job remains a barrier to women's advancement into the leadership of public agencies and private corporations. For the foreseeable future, authorities like *Fortune* magazine will continue to tell women who aspire to organizational leadership, "Look like a lady, act like a man, work like a dog" (Fierman, 1990, p. 62).

Leadership and Public Administration

To conclude this chapter, my brief against using our supposed need for public sector leadership to argue for the legitimacy of public administration is that our images of leadership are not only limited to traits many of which are associated with white professional males but also result in material disadvantage to those who appear to depart from them. We have a circular situation in which men (almost always white men) occupy the top organizational jobs; we look to current leaders for our ideas about what and who leaders are; these ideas serve as filters, screening out everyone but those who meet the accepted standards; therefore, the leaders remain the same and so do the standards. When those who are different do manage to attain a leadership position, they face a continual struggle to deal with the disparity between what people expect of leaders and what is expected of them because of characteristics like sex and race. As we saw was the case with expertise, the leadership argument privileges masculine qualities over feminine ones and supports a distribution of labor in which people who are not white professional males are at a disadvantage.

In addition, as Chapter 3 concluded with respect to expertise, arguments about the need for public sector leadership and how public administrators fill the bill reflect an effort to deny structural features of public administration that reflect culturally feminine qualities. As Rohr (1986, 1989) points out, members of the executive branch—at least those who exercise any significant amount of administrative discretion—are both leaders and clerks. They carry out orders but they also give them. The legislature, courts, and chief executive are the masters of public administrators, who are expected to be subservient to them; but "The Public Administration" frequently has the option to choose which master it will obey. Rohr's discussion of this dual nature is more explicit than most about the need for subservience on the part of public administrators; more typically, public administrators are told they must "not be weak or subservient" (Terry, 1990, p. 407). Taking orders is seen as weakness. Although awareness of it may not always be conscious, those who prototypically give orders are white males, and those who take them are women and people of color. When subjected to an analysis on the basis of gender, the image of the public servant remains paradoxical—claimed for its high moral tone, yet resisted due to its silent femininity. If this were not so, we would be discussing various arguments for the legitimacy of public administration based on its faithful obedience to the people, or the motherliness with which it keeps the public's house. In actuality, much of the work of public agencies does not involve significant exercise of discretionary power but simply the execution of routine, unglamorous, but necessary duties—work much like housework, and like it, undervalued.

Looking through the lens of gender, the entire notion of leadership—and our purported need for it—is subject to question. Rather than accepting the idea that people need someone to look up to or to tell them what to do, some theorists have asked why this appears to be so and suggested that perhaps under other circumstances leadership might not seem so necessary, or, more accurately, we might see leadership differently. We might see it as a necessary coordinating role that many, if not most, organizational members are perfectly capable of fulfilling, a position that is occupied by any one member only temporarily. Ferguson (1984) has suggested that perhaps leadership should consist as much (maybe more) in being at the center of a network of relationships as it does in being at the top of a pyramid. Astin and Leland (1991) see leadership as inherently a social change process that puts a premium on the empowerment of others and the creation of networks for joint effort. Because most of us have so little experience with any such arrangements and because business as usual seems so firmly entrenched, most such ideas are dismissed as terribly impractical. I take up this question again in Chapter 7. For now, regardless of how practical or impractical alternatives may be, the idea of leadership remains deeply gendered and fundamentally problematic for women. This should be enough to reopen the question of how worthy a basis it is for defending the legitimacy of the administrative state.

5

The Hero Factory
The Dilemma of Virtue

The rectitude of public servants is an enduring concern, not just in the literature of public administration but in the world of government and politics and among the American people at large. Much of what is written and said about the moral status of public administrators is either skeptical or hortatory: Muckrakers, in time-honored fashion, go after the sloth and corruption of bureaucrats while ethicists seek to fashion moral arguments that will inspire worthy administrative behavior. Normative public administration theory, on the other hand, focuses as much on asserting the virtue of public administrators as on trying to guide or find fault with it. Although defenders of public administration recognize imperfections in the practice of administrative morality, they argue that the essence of public service lies in commitment to the common good and that public administrators are due a certain amount of respect for their willingness to make that commitment. According to this perspective, the legitimacy of administrative authority can be traced to the public-spiritedness of its exercise, which—if only citizens become aware of it—will win their support of their government and thus preserve the polity. This logic echoes Alexander Hamilton's reasoning in *Federalist 27* that the people's "confidence in and obedience to a government, will commonly be proportioned to the goodness or badness of its administration" (Cooke, 1961, p. 172). Although the apologists recognize the shortcomings of public administrators, then, they believe it important to emphasize their civic virtue in order to maintain, or win back, "the respect and attachment of the community" (Cooke, 1961, p. 173).

Many of the arguments linking the legitimacy of public administration to the virtue of administrators also echo Hamilton in their view of the people as the ultimate source of governmental authority but in need of protection against their own errors and delusions. As White (1948) pointed out, the Federalists "accepted the philosophy of government for the people, but not government by the people. In their view, government could only be well conducted if it was in the hands of the superior part of mankind—superior in education, in economic standing, and in native ability" (p. 508). Now, as then, it seems, discussions of virtue occasionally cross the fine line between asserting the rectitude of public administrators and claiming their moral superiority to the people at large.

Four images of the virtuous public administrator mark the arguments I consider in this chapter: the guardian or trustee or steward of regime values; the seeker after fame and honor; the hero; and the citizen. Once again, I will draw attention to the gender dilemmas these images raise, not only because they are culturally masculine but also because they contribute to keeping women at a disadvantage both in society and within public administration itself. In contrast to the discussions of expertise and leadership, however, the exploration of ideas about virtue in public administration will bring to light the extent to which in American political and social history virtue has been considered a feminine quality. I will suggest that the perceived femininity of virtue has contributed to its continued status as a private rather than a civic notion, and that the assertive masculinity marking images of virtue in public administration reflect an attempt, albeit unconscious, to counteract associations with womanly benevolence. As a prelude to analyzing the images themselves, I begin with a brief review of the idea of virtue in the history of American political thought. The chapter concludes with a few reflections on what the gender dilemmas surrounding ideas of virtue appear to imply about the legitimacy of public administration.

Virtue

In the arguments under consideration, the administrator's public-spiritedness wins the esteem of citizens and fosters public virtue. The virtuous public administrator not only protects and upholds the public interest but serves as an exemplar of virtue to others (see Cooper & Wright, 1992) and is qualified to educate the public to greater public spiritedness (Gawthrop, 1984) or to the practice of benevolence (Frederickson & Hart, 1985). The virtue of public administrators is public in the sense that they act on behalf of the people and because they do so visibly, if not to the eyes of the people themselves then certainly to those of elected representatives. The public administrator's virtue is strikingly performative. In carrying out their responsibilities, public administrators display the content of their individual characters to all observers and spur some, at least, to nobler aims—virtue "by contagion," Hume called it (Wills, 1984, p. 115).

The idea of virtue is the product of a long developmental process. Over more than 2,000 years, the meaning of the word *virtue* has undergone a number of transformations (Cooper, 1992). For Aristotle, virtue entailed wide-ranging excellences of character, including moral ones, which could be cultivated and which produced a balanced person capable of leading the good (therefore public) life. The character trait emphasis is also found in the four cardinal virtues of the classical period: prudence, justice, temperance, and courage; the Christian era added three theological virtues: faith, hope, and love. During the Enlightenment, Hume made virtue synonymous with obeying laws or moral rules rather than with specific character traits. By the time of the Federalists, a view of human nature as turbulently passionate and in need of control made the idea of virtue as an aspect of character seem undependable, unless it was equated with desire for fame on the part of the better sort (see below); thus the framers of the Constitution perceived the need for a governmental structure that would supply "the defect of better motives" so that "interest would do the work of virtue."

Notions of class also infected the Federalists' understanding of virtue, which in their eyes was linked to the concept of the gentleman. The gentleman of Elizabethan England, an ideal that subsequently reached America, was a man of virtue, learning, and wealth; occasionally, theory allowed that wealth was less important than virtue and learning, but in practice the three were inextricably joined, as this observation from John Adams suggests:

> The people, in all nations, are naturally divided into two sorts, the gentlemen and the simplemen. . . . By gentlemen are not meant the rich or the poor, the high-born or the low-born, the industrious or the idle; but all those who have received a liberal education. . . . We must nevertheless

remember that *generally* those who are rich, and descended from families in public life, will have the best education in arts and sciences, and therefore the gentleman will ordinarily be the richer, and born of more notable families. (quoted in White, 1948, p. 548)

The current interest in virtue on the part of public administration scholars represents a return to a fuller understanding than the one that moved the framers; it includes a developmental view of humanity and a set of positive qualities instead of a fixed notion of human nature that relies heavily on adherence to laws or rules. The modern version is intended to be open to all human beings and not just well-educated males of good family. Within this renewal of the idea of virtue, however, is an unexamined assumption. The virtue under discussion—good citizenship, or willingness to put the common good ahead of personal interests—is *public* virtue. Because Western culture since ancient Greece has associated the public with men and the private with women, an association that barred women from public life for more than two millennia, the idea of public virtue as a model for public administration deserves a bit more scrutiny.

According to Bloch (1987), the idea of public virtue in the Revolutionary period drew on both classical republican and Protestant traditions. Within classical Republicanism, virtue was a public quality fostered in a society characterized by property holding and mixed government; the virtue of the propertied was expressed in their participation in ruling, whereas that of the people at large showed itself in popular rising against invasion or corruption and in loyalty to the regime. Within Protestantism, virtue came from faith and was mainly a trait of good rules; other members of the community simply obeyed the rules and lived according to moral strictures. Both traditions, however, agreed that public virtue was masculine, while the private Christian virtues were seen as accessible equally to both sexes. The masculinity of the republican version was particularly pronounced, derived as it was from the Homeric idea of excellence tied to physical courage in battle and from Greek and Roman notions about cooperative endeavor among male citizens of the state. The masculinity of virtue is visible in Machiavelli's republican thinking. By taking political action, men achieve mastery over circumstances—that is, they outwit *fortuna*, a woman (Pitkin, 1984). Such understandings were reinforced throughout much of Western history by laws that barred women from public life; thus their significance was not just attitudinal.

During the 1780s and 1790s, according to Bloch (1987), a uniquely feminine understanding of public spiritedness began to emerge. According to the terms of *republican motherhood*, women could partake of public virtue by encouraging it in their husbands and fostering it in their sons (see also Kerber, 1980). This ideology fixed the wellspring of virtue in the home rather than in the public space itself; therefore, it supported a political shift away from reliance on the efforts of free men participating together and toward the establishment of a constitutional order that put little weight on such participation and in fact restricted it. This shift "made it possible to preserve the notion of public virtue while at the same time divesting it of its former constitutional significance" (Bloch, 1987, p. 56). Thus, whether consciously or not, the idea of home as the source of virtue supported the Federalist position: Letting "interest do the work of virtue" in public became acceptable because virtue could be seen as doing its work in the private sphere.

The purpose of the Constitution was to promote private virtues (as well as individual liberty), not public ones. Virtue became "ever more difficult to distinguish from private benevolence, personal manners, and female sexual propriety" (Bloch, 1987, p. 56). In practical terms, what public virtue remained consisted only of voting and a vague allegiance to the idea of the country, as it became symbolized in the flag and celebrated on public holidays. The confinement of virtue to domestic and social activity increasingly made it seem feminine and blurred the moral distinction between men's political activities and their self-interested economic pursuits. It became more and more difficult to expect (or at least to assume) that political behavior was driven by public spiritedness rather than the hope of individual gain.[1] Masculinity became associated less with living the good public life than with the rational pursuit of self-interest, whether in business or in government, an association that contributed to the perception of self-interest as an inevitable or natural aspect of society outside the home. During the 19th century (as the next chapter sets forth in detail), the femininity associated with ideas of virtue persisted, reinforced by cultural distinctions drawn between two modes of public life—the ostensibly masculine world of party politics and women's "private" charitable work, aimed at helping families in need.

The entrance of women into the fullness of American political life beginning in 1920, and their subsequent infiltration into elected office and into public bureaucracy, reduced neither the sharp distinction still made between public life and the domestic work of home and family nor women's disparate responsibility for the latter. Thus the current attempt in public administration at resuscitating a substantive interpretation of public virtue is a matter of going against what is still the prevailing flow. Not only must such a project combat the reigning idea that all public activity is self-interested but it must face the continuing association of virtue with femininity. Since the days of republican motherhood, virtue in America has been largely associated with private behavior. It is a quality fostered in (and largely confined to) women's sphere, one that typically has to do with female sexual, maternal, or charitable behavior and is therefore seen as weak in comparison to the tough-mindedness and realism expected of public figures. Rhetoric about heroes and guardians notwithstanding, it appears that it will be difficult either to legitimate public administration on the basis of its virtue or to foster virtue in public administrators (or other public figures) as long as people consciously or unconsciously associate virtue with femininity and as long as they fear being seen as feminine—a fear shared by both men and women involved in public life. Founder John Adams once observed, "The people are Clarissa"—that is, the people's virtue is passive and feminine—"destined to be deceived and violated by unscrupulous men in power" (quoted in Bloch, 1987, p. 57). We are in need of an understanding of virtue that is strong without being muscular, active without being competitive, laudable without elitism, selfless without passivity—given the gender dilemmas in our current notions of virtue, a tall order indeed. The following sections explore these dilemmas.

The Guardian

Many defenders of public administration invoke the idea of the guardian, trustee, or steward of public values. We encountered this idea in connection with the notion of professional autonomy (Chapter 3). There it was reflected in the Blacksburg perspective (Wamsley et al., 1990), which sees the public administrator as a trustee of the public interest and the public agency as a repository of time-tested wisdom; in Kass's (1990) steward, working on behalf of others; and in Terry's (1990) conservator of administrative capacity. In considering the virtue of public administrators, the aspect of these images on which I want to focus shifts from the autonomy they confer to their moral status as *protector*. Morgan and Kass (1991) summarize this argument:

> The stewardship model contends that the public administrator's highest duty is to protect and nurture the constitutional system of the republic and the constitutive values which the system is meant to realize. The justification for performing this role rests on two considerations that, taken together, seek both to legitimate and limit the exercise of discretionary authority by nonelected career officials. First, administrative agents take an oath to uphold our constitutional order. Second, administrative bodies possess a unique capacity to carry out this oath in a manner that furthers constitutional values. (pp. 45–46)

Here Morgan and Kass suggest that, as a result of having taken an oath of office, public administrators are more actively committed to the public interest than the general public and that they and their agencies are better qualified to decide in particular circumstances how to translate constitutional values into specific actions. Frederickson and Hart (1985) also see the public administrator as a protector. They "define the primary moral obligation of the public service in this nation as the patriotism of benevolence"; they equate this with protection of "all the people within our political boundaries . . . in all of the basic rights granted to them by the enabling documents" (p. 549). These arguments see public administrators as guardians of the polity and of the individual rights of its members.

The elitism of the idea of guardianship—always possible, sometimes actual—has been pointed out (e.g., Fox & Cochran, 1990). Yet the idea persists that citizens are in need of protection not only from the depredations of those who would deprive them of their rights but also from the results of their own selfishness, ignorance, and irrationality. From this perspective, the people are not only the vulnerable Clarissa but also the headstrong Emma, in need of chastening, or the shrewish Kate, in need of taming. It is difficult to appeal to the idea of guardianship without calling forth an attendant cluster of images that render those being guarded either helpless or dangerous. The protectors of rights can too easily become protectors against the efforts of the possessors of rights to protect themselves. The people are asked to trust trustees who do not trust them. The age-old question—Who will guard the guardians?—is relevant here. To those outside the system of government, the checks, balances, separated powers, and other restraints on administrative power pale beside their own sense of vulnerability to it.

The gender dilemma in the guardian image should be apparent. The public space is historically a male preserve and the work of statesmanship a masculine effort to tame *fortuna* and control the archetypically feminine, unruly people. Guardians are paternal figures—heads of the public household—who tell other members, perhaps gently but certainly firmly, what is best for them. The public spiritedness of the protected people, like the virtue of women, lies in obedience and loyalty. The significance of the guardian image is as an effort to instill masculinity in the idea of virtue, to make it strong by making it fatherly. I should note that Morgan and Kass's (1991) analysis contains within it the potential for a less paternal rendering of the guardian, in their reference to the protector as nurturer and to public administrators as "midwives of change." I explore these ideas in Chapter 7. For now, it is enough to note that the masculinity of the guardian image—the first of our four models of virtue—makes it a problem for women in the administrative state; longstanding expectations about the private nature of women's proper role and sphere are inconsistent with the image of public guardian.

The Seeker After Fame and Honor

I'm Nobody! Who are you?
Are you—Nobody—Too?
Then there's a pair of us?
Don't tell! they'd advertise—you know!

How dreary—to be—Somebody!
How public—like a Frog—
To tell one's name—the livelong June—
To an admiring bog!

—Emily Dickinson (in Johnson, 1960, p. 133)

The framers of the Constitution envisaged a system in which the work of government would be carried on by the better sort—by virtuous and educated gentlemen. They did not expect all such men to be naturally attracted to the burdens of public office; in fact, they knew that such responsibilities were at best a mixed blessing. In 1816, John Adams advised a young friend,

You must steel your heart and prepare your mind to encounter multitudes of political enemies, and to endure all the buffetings without which there is no rising to distinction in the American world. When the knaves and fools open upon you in full pack, take little or no notice of them; and be careful not to lose your temper. Preserve your private character and reputation unsullied, and confine your speculations upon public concerns to objects of high and national importance. (quoted in White, 1951, pp. 197–198n.)

What the founders believed would induce men of talent and character to endure the difficulties of governing the republic was the desire for fame and honor, which they considered a noble motive. It was an idea with a long history: In the Roman era, for example, Cicero observed that "public esteem is the nurse of the arts and all men are fired to application by fame" (quoted in Braudy, 1986, p. 56). But at the time of the founding, the passion for fame and honor had a special meaning. According to Adair's (1974) account, the desire for fame involved acting "before an audience of the wise and the good"; it is "a noble passion because it can transform ambition and self-interest into dedicated effort for the community" (p. 11)—thus it harmonizes with the framers' intent to let interest do the work of virtue. The related desire for honor, Adair tells us, while also worthy is somewhat less noble because its connotation of "dignity appropriate to . . . state" (p. 11) makes it inherently exclusive; the Virginia gentleman's code of honor, Adair argues, was able to encompass chattel slavery and treatment of women as intellectual inferiors. For Adair, the passion for fame is particularly commendable because of its public character; essentially it is the desire of "a man to make history, to leave the mark of his deeds and his ideals on the world" (p. 11). Mainzer (1964), on the other hand, sees honor as a mixture of "inner quality and public judgment" that has a "peculiarly social basis" because "the standards for determining honor are communal" (p. 71). But he also finds honor flawed in its class bias and observes that "for women it has been largely confined to chastity—virginity before marriage, fidelity thereafter" (p. 72). Richardson and Adkins (1997) note that ideas of honor are insulated from challenge by the life of privilege that aristocrats lead.

Green (1988) has suggested that modern public administrators, as "prudent constitutionalists," are—and should be—motivated by the desire for fame and honor. Green argues that those who "love the fame of laudable actions" can be entrusted with "great powers" over long periods of time because "their most passionate interests connect with their virtue, and coincide with the duties of office." The result is "a level of insularity sufficient to instill a sense of ownership in the duties of office, and a degree of detachment necessary for exercising wise judgment" (p. 38). Without such powers, which are the prerequisite for attracting an audience of the wise and for leaving one's mark on history, the public administrator may become irresponsible. Linked to power is the prudent constitutionalist's "fair and virtuous independence"; even though public administrators—even department heads—are subordinates, their devotion to regime values and to the public good in general legitimates a measure of autonomy appropriate to their role as policymakers. Green contrasts this subordinate independence with what he sees as current stress on a combination of neutral competence and blind loyalty to the political leader. Finally, administrators with due regard for fame and reputation will invest a great deal of themselves in their work. They will seek sufficient time and power to realize their plans and policies. In our regime, this requires a great deal of cooperation among the separate powers. Sustained cooperation rests ultimately on the maintenance of "moral understandings or gentlemen's agreements" (p. 44; material in quotation marks from Louis Fisher). Green concludes that administrators who are willing to make the necessary investment of time and energy in their work will, indeed, "leave the imprint of their character" on their duties (p. 45).

Green's image of the prudent constitutionalist echoes and builds on Alexander Hamilton's ideas about what it would take to make the new government work—in particular, Hamilton's theory that sound administration, by which Hamilton meant administration with real clout, would win the hearts and minds of the people away from excessive attachment to the rival state governments. Sound administration would require men of the better sort, attracted to public service by the prospect of winning public fame. Studies of Hamilton (Adair, 1974; Caldwell, 1988) confirm Green's (1988) assessment of Hamilton as "one of our greatest public administrators" (p. 25). They also portray Hamilton as exceedingly concerned about acquiring fame and leaving his own mark on history. For example, Caldwell (1988) notes, "Tinctured with vanity and a romantic urge to fame, [Hamilton's] purpose was to do some work of truly historic significance" (p. 3). He observes that Hamilton argued for a single head of each department on the basis that "men of the first pretensions will not so readily engage in [boards], because they will be less conspicuous, of less importance, have less opportunity of distinguishing themselves" (p. 45).

Because his ambition was coupled with one of the best analytical minds of his age, Hamilton's life was marked by accomplishments of a scale that ensured that his dream of leaving his imprint on history came true. Before adopting Hamilton as an exemplary image for virtuous public administration, however, perhaps we should explore the gender dilemmas in the Hamiltonian image of the public administrator as seeker after fame and honor. We might begin by noting the nature of Hamilton's own exemplars. Adair (1974) points out that Hamilton, when selecting pseudonyms for certain of his political pamphlets (a common practice at the time), picked men of heroic virtue from Greek and Roman history (Phocion, Tully, Camillus, and Pericles) who shared "a profound contempt for the people whom they rule and serve so devotedly"; moreover, all four "in their biographies are seen to be misjudged, betrayed, persecuted by the miserable populace whose safety and well-being depend on the superman's abilities and services to the state" (pp. 276–278). Hamilton's principal hero, Adair observes, was Julius Caesar, whom he knew through reading Plutarch:

> Plutarch's Caesar is the hero of the world's most sinister success story—a man of transcendant genius who could find self-fulfillment only in the exercise of unchecked power over his fellows. . . . His "love of honor and passion for distinction" led him to court dangers in battle from which his rank would have normally exempted him. Conscious of his genius and certain of what he most desired, he recognized in the social instability and political disorders of Rome the typical revolutionary circumstances which could be exploited in his own pursuit of power, a power which would be used to restore social order and gain him immortal fame. (p. 279)

Finding a number of striking parallels between Julius Caesar's career and Hamilton's own, Adair concludes that Hamilton secretly aimed to succeed George Washington, an ambition that warped his judgment on certain issues and might have led him to "attempt the short and easy way of usurpation of power outside the constitution" if the right circumstances had presented themselves. Acknowledging the need for further research into Hamilton, Adair comments, "No matter how tentatively we say it, until more evidence comes to light, Hamilton would appear to be a statesman who could thus be described in neoclassical rhetoric: 'Curse on his virtues; they have *almost* undone his country'" (p. 284).

Looking through the lens of gender, what are we to make of the Hamiltonian public administrator, the seeker after fame, honor, and reputation, the maker of a mark on history, the actor before an audience of the wise and the good? We have already seen that even nonfeminist scholars note the cultural masculinity of the notions of fame and honor. Mainzer (1964) observes that the concept of honor is generally inapplicable to women and criticizes its excessive "brutality," which he says leads us to ignore the gentler aspects of our natures. Adair (1974) notes that the Virginia gentlemen's code of honor did not keep them from owning slaves or from looking on women as inferior.

In addition, we encountered in previous chapters certain other difficulties connected with fame and honor. For example, the masculine concern for detachment and independence that I discussed in connection with the interest in autonomy, both for the professional administrator and for the administrator as leader, is evidenced here as well. Lerner (1986) notes that "The very concept of honor, for men, embodies autonomy, the power to . . . decide for oneself," a power that even privileged white women, let alone poor women of color, have rarely had under patriarchal rule, where they have generally been restricted to the home and their bodies have been at the disposal of their husbands and fathers—or owners and masters (p. 80).[2]

To make one's mark, to be noticed by the wise and good audience, requires independence; one's accomplishments must not disappear into the work of the agency but be singled out for approbation. As we saw in Chapter 3, the masculine desire for autonomy is in tension with the feminine expectation of responsiveness. Green (1988) argues, as did Hamilton (and Woodrow Wilson, for that matter) that administrators are both independent and subordinate and that "large powers" promote rather than impede responsibility because of the Hamiltonian administrator's desire for visibility. Green's is a rather paternal if not Olympian notion of responsibility, however, one that includes winning the people's loyalty by protecting them against their own impulses and delusions, thus one that deals with the need for feminine responsiveness by projecting it outward in order to retain the desired independence. Mainzer (1964) notes that personal responsibility and critical ethical thinking are necessary if honor is to be a moral notion:

> For independent, vital expression one must be outside or on top, not a subordinate. . . . If day after day, over years, one is treated as a

subordinate in one of the most important functions of his life, this may affect whatever is most basic and continuing about a person. . . . Bettelheim found that to survive as a man, though degraded, in the concentration camps, it was necessary to remain aware of the point beyond which a man would never give in, whatever the price, and to remain aware of one's attitudes toward and reasons for compliance. (pp. 86–88)

Mainzer means to draw attention here to the to the difficulty of constructing bureaucratic behavior as morally responsible. As a woman, however, one cannot read such a passage without reflecting on all the women who have spent their lives not "outside or on top" but inside or on the bottom, treated as subordinates in every aspect of their lives, and told that their status was worthy (but only for them). Of course, Mainzer has a point: Few *men* have actually spent much time on top of their organizations, but manhood per se has never disqualified them from trying.

We have also encountered (in the discussion of the profession as a brotherhood) Green's (1988) idea that Hamiltonian administrators must invest themselves heavily in their work; that discussion pointed out the difficulty for most women in making this sort of investment—how their responsibilities for home life and child rearing tend to preclude their having the same freedom that men do to throw themselves head over heels into their careers. Thus the Hamiltonian image must be problematic for women because of its paternalism and for its basis in a totality of commitment to work that many, if not most, women find it hard to achieve.

There are a number of additional issues to be raised. One is the psychological assumptions on which the Hamiltonian image is premised. The view of human nature that Hamilton (and most other Federalists) espoused includes the presumption of self-interest coupled with personal ambition. Clearly, the supposition that self-interest is the wellspring of virtually all human action is challenged by ideas of maternal love and wifely responsibility for the household; something other than self-interest must lie behind women's willingness to devote so much of their lives to their husbands and children—a willingness on which is predicated the entire liberalist division of life into public and domestic spheres. Personal ambition, too, while not as universalized an assumption as self-interest, ill suits ordinary notions of what animates the lives of women. As we saw was true of the idea of leadership, on a common-sense level ambition is associated with masculinity. In addition, some recent research suggests that women tend not to be driven by the need for external recognition. For example, Markus (1987) found that the women she studied equated achievement with the accomplishment of specific objectives and saw success in private terms such as gaining self-confidence, obtaining credentials under tough circumstances, or coping with their double roles. Markus suggests that only by changing the dominant definition of success (that is, recognition achieved through the single-minded pursuit of a full-time career) will women be able to "succeed" (I would add, and to gain fame and honor). She notes,

> Such a change would mean . . . that women would be able to cease being the "sole repository for repressed human values," that is, they would be able not only to overcome the limitations of the socially ascribed "gender role" but also to bring into public life those behavioral and emotional patterns that are exclusively ascribed to them but which are [now] applicable only in the private sphere. (p. 107)

She cautions, however (quoting Ellen Goodman), "It is easier to dress for success than to change the meaning of success" (p. 107).[3]

The publicness of the idea of fame is also problematic because, like every other aspect of the Western idea of the public sphere, it is predicated on the existence of a domestic sphere to which lowly concerns like food, shelter, clothing, and reproduction of the species are consigned along with the women responsible for them. To be in the public sphere is to act before an audience, to see and be seen, an idea that dates back to ancient Greece. Braudy (1986) notes that "in such a theatrical conception of life, when seeing someone from the outside constitutes the most accurate and authentic perspective, the offstage is the obscene" (p. 38).

The desire to make one's distinctive mark on history is also part of the publicness of the quest for fame; in essence, this represents a longing for immortality. The activities that form the quest are themselves a rejection of bodily concerns in favor of more lofty issues—that is, those of the mind: in public administrative terms, a repudiation of ministerial considerations in favor of policymaking and the exercise of discretionary authority. The hoped-for result of these efforts, however—to go down in history and therefore to cheat death—represents the ultimate triumph over the body. Brown's (1988) study finds this theme running through the course of Western political thought, beginning in ancient Greece. She notes that the Greeks both disdained and glorified the body. On the one hand, they praised those bodies that appeared to surpass human limits of beauty or physical prowess. But they equated the ordinary body with animality and—because women seemed to them to be particularly entrapped in their bodies—with femininity; women were therefore seen as threats to men's human freedom and potentiality. Brown observes,

> The Platonic dualism of "being" vs. "becoming" . . . reveals Greek man's conception of the threat posed to his freedom by nature and by the nature he ascribed to women. In politics and philosophy, man strives toward Being (a state occupied by the gods and all immortals) and to escape the mire of Becoming. Becoming is a condition Socrates described as a "barbaric bog.". . . Becoming, Nature, and Woman are . . . linked to one another and appear to stand for danger and subversion in the mind of the Greek man. His fear of falling into this barbaric bog was addressed through heroic political and military feats and through zealous pursuit of rational truth. The fear of being pulled into this state was dealt with by casting nature and necessity as contaminating, as matter in need of form, and above all, as subject to man's mastery. (pp. 56–57)

Richardson and Adkins's (1997) meditation on the novel *King Rat*, by James Clavell, and its lessons for public administration, brings out the long-standing equation of nature and the body with women and civilization with men. The novel, which deals with British, American, and Australian inmates of a Japanese prison camp during World War II, highlights this nature-nurture division by stripping it away, presenting the reader with a setting in which conventions like clothes, class distinctions, and modesty are gone, leaving qualities of "manhood," such as cunning and "luck," to differentiate among the prisoners (p. 208). Ironically, however, in a world without women, civilization itself disappears (one of the characters says that "without women . . . men are a cruel joke" [p. 218, n. 11]). Also ironically, in the all-male milieu the only source of "fame" comes from taking on the role of a female, first in camp theatrics, then at large; in these cases, say the authors, "the age-old tension between nature—specifically the malleability of human nature—and nurture is artfully held up to the reader's gaze" (p. 205). Ultimately, however, for the authors the value of the parable is to show how when bodily survival is at stake and all distinctions of class or profession have vanished, each man still has the chance to "know his own character as it truly is" (p. 204)—thus, once again, to rise above bodily survival in the sense that it is no longer the most important factor in deciding what to do.

Brown (1988) argues that the quest to "rise above" the body is a politically pernicious one because it is used to support policies in aid of a national interest said to require the sacrifice of domestic concerns (those dearest to the hearts of women because of their life experiences), frequently even the literal sacrifice of lives. A secondary result, of course, is that through the equation of women with lesser bodily concerns—those over which the national interest takes precedence—a woman's quest for fame and immortality is fraught with the same tensions as we saw in the cases of professionalism and leadership. Culturally and ideologically, women represent the "barbaric bog"—or perhaps, according to the epigraph heading this section, Emily Dickinson's "admiring bog"—while men are the seekers after pure Being (Dickinson's "public frogs"). Stereotypically, women have spent their lives saying, "I'm nobody! Who are you?" and taking vicarious pleasure in the accomplishments of their husbands and sons. In actuality, only a relatively small proportion of women have husbands and sons with a real chance at fame and honor, but the force of the stereotype is more widely felt and blocks the efforts of many different women to identify with this image and to be identified with it by others. The image of the Hamiltonian administrator—in its stress on autonomy, detachment, and independence, in its assumptions of self-interest and ambition, in its publicness, and in its orientation toward disembodiedness—is fraught with gender dilemmas.

The Hero

A central part of the legitimation effort among public administration theorists in recent years has been the presentation of exemplary figures: real public administrators, living or dead, who embody what is most praiseworthy about public service. One objective of this effort is to show the public at large how laudable the practice of public administration can be; another is to raise the spirits and spur the efforts of civil servants themselves, who have borne the brunt of particularly heavy criticism from all quarters (including presidential) over the past few decades. The idea behind recounting the lives of exemplars is that contemplation of the lives of people struggling toward moral excellence in familiar circumstances engages the emotions and makes us want to strive toward virtue in a way that analysis and the formulation of codes of ethics cannot (Cooper & Wright, 1992).

Bellavita (1991) put a distinctive twist on the exemplar by arguing for the notion of the public administrator as hero. Bellavita questioned a group of midlevel federal bureaucrats about their "personal best organizational experiences." He found that the ways in which administrators characterize their experiences conformed to what Joseph Campbell called the *hero's journey*, a story that takes the form of call to adventure, ordeal, and return. Bellavita uses the framework of the hero's journey to present the stories of several practitioners, with the aim of offering guidance to other public administrators.

Bellavita (1991) suggests that a public administrator undertakes the hero's journey out of a sense of duty, the opportunity to "test an idea or act on a belief" (p. 160) and "the drive to achieve something tangible and meaningful" (p. 161). Although the administrative hero, like Campbell's archetype, "has helpers along the way, the journey is fundamentally an individual and voluntary undertaking" (p. 162). The moral import of the hero is found in the willingness to sacrifice "some part of the self for an ideal that is bigger than self. The sacrifice may be time, friendships, reputation, family, career, or on rare occasions life" (p. 174).

As was the case with the guardian and the seeker after fame and honor, the image of the public administrator as hero is a dubious one for women. Terry (1991) has already criticized the hero idea; he asks whether public administration is "so hungry for positive images . . . that we devour them whole" (p. 2) and points to the negative aspects of the hero as the image has come down to us from Homeric times—the hero's violence and recklessness, self-centeredness, stubbornness, and symbolism of male dominance. Although Bellavita (1991) does suggest that the hero image is applicable to both men and women, his optimism on this point is belied by the structural masculinity of the hero concept in ancient times, when it took the form in which it has come down to us. Finley (1965) states that "'hero' has no feminine gender in the age of heroes" (p. 25). He points out that the hero's code, based on physical prowess and honor, admitted no rational discussion of alternatives and included no social obligations—in fact, "the community could grow only by taming the hero and blunting the free exercise of his prowess" (p. 125). In the hero's world,

the inferior status of women was neither concealed nor idealized. . . . In fact, from Homer to the end of Greek literature there were no ordinary words with the specific meanings "husband" and "wife." A man was a man, a father, a warrior, a nobleman, a chieftain, a king, a hero; linguistically, he was almost never a husband. (p. 136)

Finley notes that wives were ordinarily referred to as "bedmates."

The question, then, as Terry (1991) suggests, is whether we can take only the positive aspects of the idea and cast aside the negative ones. Certainly, to advocate that we do so implies that our use of symbols and images is driven by conscious rationality, a proposition that I think Campbell himself, as a Jungian, would have rejected. In addition, one's own self-identity affects the ease with which it is possible to pick and choose aspects of images or to judge certain features as marginal to their impact or relatively unimportant to our assessment of overall moral worth.

As an example, consider Blum's (1988) treatment of Oskar Schindler, made famous by Thomas Keneally's *Schindler's List* and the award-winning movie by Steven Spielberg. Schindler was a factory owner who, at great personal risk, saved thousands of Jews during World War II. Blum's article turns to Schindler as a moral exemplar; his analysis judges Schindler a "moral hero" despite his having been a "libertine" and a man with two mistresses in addition to a wife. Blum's argument is premised on the assumption that private (domestic) behavior is less morally salient than public. He maintains that to disqualify Schindler on the basis of his sexual exploits would constitute a "denial of sensuality and sexuality . . . difficult to justify in terms of the broader perspective of concern for human well-being" (p. 200). Blum suggests that since sexual activity is necessary for physical and emotional health, we must resist faulting Schindler for infidelity. Blum says that, even though Schindler's extramarital activities apparently pained his wife, they do not eliminate him out of hand as an exemplar; we would "have to know more about the specific nature" of their relationship. Blum comments, "There is no suggestion that Oskar mistreated Emelie" (p. 200). Blum neglects to tell us what we would have to know about the Schindlers' marriage to make Oskar's infidelity morally acceptable despite the fact that it pained his wife; evidently, Blum does not consider the behavior that caused this pain mistreatment. Blum concludes that Schindler's sexual behavior makes him "less of a moral paragon than he would otherwise be; but he remains, I think, a moral hero" (p. 200).

The assessment of Schindler seems to me, however, a more perplexing project than Blum makes it—I continue to think so, despite the fact that my argument concerning Schindler elicited more negative comments than any other element in the first edition of this book. Like these criticisms, Blum's assessment appears to be based on the assumption that sexual transgressions—for example, the breaking of a trust between husband and wife—are less important to a person's overall moral worth than willingness to risk one's life to save the lives of others. He and the critics may be right—but is the one so much less significant than the other that we are safe in calling such a man a moral hero? Part of my reluctance to discount Schindler's sexual behavior started with a sense that the dividing line between public and domestic realms has had the effect, historically, of rendering men's domination and mistreatment of women relatively marginal to the assessment of their characters. Yet the impeachment of President Bill Clinton on the basis of sexual misconduct and of his reluctance to come clean about it suggests that in at least one sense the public-private line is beginning to blur—not, unfortunately however, in a way that serves the cause of equality between men and women. As Dobel (1998) points out, weakening accepted notions about the privacy of private life threatens women even more than men, since women "cannot rely on patterns of acceptance or rituals of public excuse or forgiveness that would enable them to escape public censure and delegitimation in the way men might to handle accusations of private impropriety" (p. 119).

My argument here is not so much with Schindler as it is with Blum, who goes too far, it seems to me, in excusing Schindler's sexual peccadillos as necessary to his health. (One wonders how all the men who have resisted cheating on their wives have managed to stay healthy.) The extraordinary thing about Schindler is not that the rest of his behavior was irrelevant to judging his moral worth but that, in spite of this behavior, he was able to rise to greatness in an extraordinary moment. In other words, Schindler is an exemplar to the rest of us precisely because of his ordinariness. He shows us that flawed human beings are capable of exceeding their limits. The significance of Schindler is not based on the paltriness of his domestic sins but on the magnitude of this one achievement; this is what separates him from Bill Clinton or Clarence Thomas, both run through the "exceeding fine" mill of media-generated public scrutiny, neither apparently able to point to deeds that could demonstrate depth of character that might outweigh the flaws in their sexual conduct.

Examining the notion of hero or exemplar through the lens of gender suggests the need to rework it entirely. First of all, we would want greater consciousness of what our choice of heroes reveals about what is important to us; many heroes in United States culture are quite literally "commanding" figures or those who succeed in intensely competitive efforts, such as generals, professional sportsmen, and business "miracle workers." The cultural masculinity of the hero image makes the female hero an anomaly, a challenge to thinking as usual (note that the *heroine* is less the doer of great deeds than the one rescued by the hero). Edwards (1984) suggests that defining heroism in terms of physical strength or social power excludes women, but that coming to see women as heroes can reshape our understanding:

> The woman hero uncovers fractures in the surface of reality. . . . Insofar as she resembles the male hero, she questions the conventional associations of gender and behavior. If . . . she can do as he has done, then patriarchy's prohibitions are a lie. . . . And when she differs from the male hero, she denies the link between heroism and either gender or behavior. (pp. 4–5)

Warner's (1981) study of Joan of Arc presents a good example of how a woman hero "fractures . . . the surface of reality." Warner argues that, because in Joan's culture male virtue meant courage while women's meant meekness, she needed a "framework of virtue" that would allow her to "marry her self-image to her actions" (p. 147); therefore, she put on armor, which both protected her against men and "attached men by aping their appearance in order to usurp their functions" (p. 155). Warner points out, however, that Joan never pretended to be a man, and the image of the young girl wearing male armor constituted a symbol that partakes of a "third order" (p. 145)—neither male nor female but embodying something of both without eclipsing either. Joan thus accomplished what Edwards (1984) suggests the woman hero does: She "upset the tyranny of social fact and revealed its contingency" (p. 237)—leaving in place, however (as Warner notes), "masculinity as the touchstone and equality a process of imitation" (p. 155).

Warner (1981) raises the key question for a gender-based reflection on the hero or exemplar: Can we have images that do not require women to "put on masculinity" in order to qualify? As I have argued elsewhere, so few women have reached positions of significant authority and power in American public life (that is, positions where they come into the public eye) that women aspiring to morally significant lives in the public sector really have little idea what—or whom—they might become (Stivers, 1992a). There is great need to examine the lives of the few women exemplars we do have from a perspective that, instead of unthinkingly measuring them against prevailing standards drawn out of men's lives, reveals their struggle to accomplish without imitating men, their need (as we saw in the discussion on leadership) to manage their femaleness, and the difficulty they have in living according to values and standards many of which the world in which they practice does not share. As we learn more about such women, it may be—as Edwards (1984) suggests—that our accepted notions of what constitutes a hero or exemplar will change.

For women in the public sector to serve as exemplars of virtue, we will have to make at least one important structural change in the way we define virtuous lives. We will have to rethink the barrier between public and domestic life. This is admittedly a thorny issue, as the discussion of Oskar Schindler shows; the terms of American political life lead us to treat discussions of private behavior as fit material only for the front pages of tabloids and opportunistic talk-show hosts. Those who long for a return to consideration of substantive issues in political debate see the obsession with the sexual exploits of politicians as a degradation of electoral politics. Yet the rule that the private lives of public figures should be off limits has costs as well as benefits—making it difficult, for example, in accounts of exemplary lives to deal with moral dilemmas raised by conflicts between public and private obligations. Are people heroes whose single-minded devotion to the public good makes them strangers to their children? Does infidelity or sexual harassment really count in our assessment of the worth of public lives? We cannot consider such questions adequately as long as we segregate moral issues into public and private, if private is to mean "relatively insignificant" or "beyond scrutiny." On the other hand, the trend toward ever more frenzied media concentration on the private lives of public figures has had the ironic effect not of strengthening the public but of driving out truly public questions from consideration. Reflecting on media obsession with the private life of Representative Gary Condit, friend of the missing intern Chandra Levy, Tom Rosenstiel of The Project for Excellence in Journalism, commented, "The real impact is not that there's no such thing as something that is private. It's that there's no such thing as public. What used to be private fills our public space. What used to be the subject of our public sphere is pushed out" (quoted in Barringer, 2001, p. 3).

We can take this discussion of moral heroes one additional step, however, to ask the question of whether we need exemplars at all. Fisher

(1988) argues that models or heroes perpetuate "the logic of domination, by encouraging us to look *up* to 'special women' rather than to look around us for the women with whom we might act" (p. 212). She observes that many women today are striving to lead lives that have no clear precedent because they break with the social roles assigned to women throughout the ages; therefore, exemplars can provide no definitive answers to the dilemmas such women face. Under such conditions, Fisher suggests, creating role models or exemplars is an act of "moral faith," a discovery process, an exploration; but "we find ourselves on a constant moral frontier in which neither our nor anyone else's experience or knowledge of the world guarantees our transition from the present to the future" (p. 217). She concludes,

> Ideal versions of other women's lives can help us in [the] search [for meaning,] but, in the end, the ways in which we present *our own* lives in talking and working with each other have an even greater impact on its outcome . . . not only our successes . . . but also the conditions that have made [them] possible and the contradictions we have failed to overcome. (p. 231, italics added)

From this perspective, we would find our exemplars not by looking up but by looking across, by listening, and by revealing ourselves to one another. We invent the future not by contemplating the marble statues of the founders that came out of 18th-century sculptor Houdon's "hero factory" (Wills, 1984) but by listening to one another's stories and working together.

The Citizen

A fourth image of the virtuous administrator is that of citizen. The major proponent is Cooper (1984a, 1984b, 1991); he argues that "the democratic legitimacy of public administration grows out of the fiduciary nature of the public administrative role. The public administrator is most fundamentally a citizen who acts on behalf of the citizenry in carrying out certain public functions" (1991, p. 4). For Cooper, the ethical obligations of the public administrator are like those of the democratic citizen; they include the practice of horizontal authority relations (power with instead of power over); a search for the public interest, a responsive form of professionalism that wields expertise under the people's sovereignty; and a continuing covenant or set of shared expectations with fellow citizens. Cooper (1991) believes that the administrator's most fundamental obligation is to preserve the practice of citizenship itself; duties like maintaining specific institutions and implementing programs are secondary. Acting as a "citizen for the rest of us," Cooper's citizen-administrator exercises authority on behalf of other citizens and becomes a "witness for the common good," calling on the community itself to become better (p. 161).

Because the energy in Cooper's conceptualization runs horizontally instead of vertically and because he emphasizes the characteristics and values that administrators and other citizens share rather than the things that set them apart, his theory is more appealing than many images of public administration. Yet there are paradoxes in the notion of citizenship that require exploring.

By now, the exclusion of women, slaves, and the foreign-born from the Athenian polity of Aristotle's day is too well known to need cataloguing here, as are the contortions that liberal theorists had to perform in order to grant women citizenship in theory while withholding it from them in practice (see Clark & Lange, 1979; Okin, 1979; Pateman, 1989; Saxonhouse, 1985). A couple of specific issues are worth pointing out, however. One is that while a central aspect of citizenship has been the right to speak, gender and ethnic background have restricted access to civic speech since ancient Greece. Only comparatively recently have women in Western democracies won the right to vote, been elected to public office, headed public agencies, and served equally on juries, and they are still markedly underrepresented in the public life of most countries relative to their numbers in the population. Similarly, the existence of citizenship ideals in societies that limit citizenship on the basis of ethnicity (including the United States under slavery and Jim Crow laws) suggests that, despite its being asserted as a universal principle, citizenship depends on exclusion—on there being "others" whose inferior status serves to exalt citizenship. As a principle, citizenship appears to require "identical" citizens, whose differences (such as gender or race) are politically insignificant, yet certain "others"—women and people of color—continue to be defined as different in order to rationalize substantive inequality. The existence of this paradox makes the image of citizenship problematic for people whose race and/or gender have long been equivocal elements in the dialogue about citizenship (Stivers, 1996b, 2000b).

A second problem with the image of the public administrator as citizen is the strict boundary between public and private realms that it appears to require. The segregation of domestic concerns outside the political leaves Woman in an equivocal position, unable to speak for the universal public interest without divesting herself of her particularity—without becoming Public Man (Landes, 1988). We have used the idea of the public interest, concern for which is a defining element of citizenship, as if the public space throughout history were equally open to men and women. In order to modify the notion of citizenship we need to unsettle the boundaries that relegate the domestic sphere into apolitical darkness. As Shklar (1991) notes, "The struggle for citizenship in America has . . . been overwhelmingly a demand for inclusion in the polity, an effort to break down excluding barriers to recognition" (p. 3).

Finally, Cooper's (1991) definition of virtuous citizenship is "self-interest rightly understood," an idea derived from Alexis de Tocqueville. Cooper's enthusiasm for this way of understanding citizenship stems, he says, from a desire to avoid the classical republican implication that the state comes first; he wants a definition that suits the modern multiplicity of roles—we are not just citizens but lots of other things as well. Therefore, he seeks an understanding that fuses public virtue with the American interest in personal development, one that does not demand sacrifice of the self to the state but, rather, entails coming to see one's own interest as interwoven with the interests of others. Enlightened self-interest is inculcated not by the state itself but in mediating institutions like family, church, school, and neighborhood association.

Cooper argues that self-interest rightly understood—if rightly understood—need not imply selfishness. He suggests that we think of the "self" in self-interest as "complex, at once familial and communitarian"; to counter the usual image of isolated, competitive individuals, he offers Sampson's notion of "ensembled individualism," in which the self has permeable boundaries open to influence by other selves and groups—a form Cooper observes is more consistent with the sense of the individual encountered in non-Western cultures and among feminists (Cooper, 1991, p. 155).

Cooper advocates self-interest rightly understood because, as he says, "self-interest seems as inescapable now as it did to de Tocqueville. The task is not to banish it but to bound and humble it" (p. 157). But from whose perspective does self-interest appear so inevitable? The apparent pervasiveness of self-interest does not hold up to careful scrutiny. Cooper notes several authors whose research has called the ubiquity of self-interest into question. He does not, however, question the roots of the assumption, which lie in culturally masculine interests like competition, autonomy, and mastery; nor does he interrogate the paradox through which an ostensibly universal human characteristic fails to extend into the "haven in a heartless world"—the home. The inculcation of self-interest rightly understood depends on the existence of a realm that does not operate on premises that it makes any sense to call "self-interest," no matter how understood.

Cooper is, in fact, battling the fallacious reasoning that begins by assuming that human nature is innately selfish and then is stuck with redefining as some hybrid variant of self-interest all the behaviors that do not look or feel self-interested. We need "self-interest rightly understood" only if all human action must be thought of as in some way self-interested, an assertion that takes on a tautological air (that is, behavior=self-interest). The familial experiences of women (and of many men also) tell them that all behavior is not self-interested. If so, then perhaps it would make more sense—and would be more transformative along the lines Cooper seeks—to find models for virtuous citizenship in the realms where, according to his theory, it is to be fostered: in the home, the school, the church, and the neighborhood association. The difficulty, of course, is the reigning viewpoint that importing ideas from the domestic or affiliative realm into the public is inappropriate—a perception that has barred for generations the ways of cultural womanhood from making any impact on public affairs (or at least any acknowledged impact). Feminist theorists have begun to make suggestions along these lines, and I consider some of them in the final chapter. For now, it is enough to point out that one cannot understand why Cooper's argument takes the form it does without understanding the masculinist roots of central ideas in Western political thought like self-interest and the division between public and private.

Conclusion

This review of the gender dilemmas in ideas of virtue in public administration has identified several counts on which they must be considered problematic. The underlying aim of these theories, to resuscitate the idea of public virtue in order to defend administrative authority, runs headlong into a gender-based division of social life into public and domestic sectors, a division that makes men primarily responsible for public affairs and women for domestic duties, and the very terms of which have respectively masculine and feminine qualities. The nature of public life is that it is populated by independent, rational, autonomous men (or women "passing" as men), who protect the common good (sometimes merely by acting as referees among various claimants to public goods) and control the impulses of the people. Actors in the public sphere perform their duties out of enlightened self-interest to win fame in the eyes of the wise and the good (each other) and to go down in history. The nature of domestic life is to support life in the public sector—to provide the material conditions that make it possible for public life to go on and to inculcate a concern for the common good. The existence of the public sector thus depends on there being another sphere in which reigning premises about human nature do not apply—one where virtue (benevolence, selflessness) rules and to which the desire for fame does not extend.

Advocates of the idea of public virtue therefore face the uphill task of bringing into public life a set of qualities that not only are thought not to apply there but are also seen as actively subversive of its premises—qualities that represent an incursion of the emotional, affiliative, selfless (therefore weak) feminine into the rational, enlightened, self-interested, autonomous masculine. It is not the idea of public virtue itself that is objectionable but the assumption that we can have it without addressing an understanding of social life that divides existence both conceptually and materially into two different realms and privileges one (and its inhabitants) over the other. Certainly, we cannot achieve public virtue as long as our images and exemplars reinforce the masculinist aspects of public life instead of undermining them. We must be willing to think new thoughts, to enter into Fisher's (1998) discovery process that makes a life that has no clear precedent, to invent the future not by building a hero factory but by building solidarity among people with similar aims, wherever we find them. We must be willing to be thought unrealistic. We must be willing to acknowledge the threads of womanhood within public administration and be prepared to weave a new fabric.

Notes

1. The class bias in the idea of virtue continued, because it was the higher ranked and not poor women who came under its sway.

2. Lest it be thought that this is a phenomenon of the ancient past, recall that only in recent times have laws in some states been altered to prohibit husbands from raping their wives.

3. Adair (1974) notes that Alexis de Tocqueville saw many of the founding fathers as worshipers at the altar of the "bitch-goddess, Success, not in the Temple of Fame" (p. 22)—which, considering the roadblocks that men have thrown in front of women's efforts to attain success on male terms, strikes one as an egregious projection and a "bum rap," indeed, on the female sex.

6

From the Ground(s) Up

Women Reformers and the Rise
of the Administrative State

Themes of expertise, leadership, and virtue on which contemporary public administration theorists rely so heavily began to emerge during the founding period of American government, when the constitutional fabric wove together strands that included the preeminence of the better sort and the need for energy in the executive. But they assumed new significance during the Progressive era, when reformers marshaled them in the interest of more active administrative government.

By focusing mainly on current-day arguments, my critiques of expertise, leadership, and virtue may have created the impression that women played no part in the historical development of these images. On this basis the reader might conclude that reframing public administration from a perspective that embraces women's needs, interests, and points of view will entail marrying two frameworks that have never been introduced to one another, so to speak. Here I want to correct that impression by reviewing highlights of the part women played during the late 19th and early 20th centuries (approximately 1880–1930), a time when the positive state developed and the self-conscious discipline of public administration took form. My aim is to suggest not only that the thinking and actions of women reformers shaped in important ways the emergence of the administrative state but also that the developing field of public administration missed opportunities to incorporate theories of the role of government and administrative action formulated by women. On the basis of historical evidence, I argue that, although the field currently assigns them little weight, women's work and thought were crucial in shaping the understanding and practice of governmental reform. Many of these unacknowledged contributions, as we will see, might be the basis for crafting new understandings of public administration, ones that not only inform administrative practice but lessen or eliminate the gender dilemmas inherent in ways we now think about it.

My view of the field of public administration as a product of Progressive reform is based on Dwight Waldo's now-classic treatment. Like Woodrow Wilson's (1887) essay "The Study of Administration," Waldo's (1948) *The Administrative State* seems to have been widely neglected upon its publication; today, however, it is almost as difficult to imagine the field without Waldo as without Wilson. Waldo conceives of public administration as an ongoing struggle to reconcile or harmonize norms of democracy and efficiency (or, to put it in other ways, participation and expertise, values and science, politics and administration). Clearly, this tension has been present since the founding era; one finds it, for example, in Hamilton's view that good government entails both "energy" (that is, effectiveness) and "safety" (or responsiveness to the people). But Waldo's analysis of Progressive thinking makes it clear that, partly because it led to a big increase in public administrative activity and partly because of the particular values it espoused, the Progressive reform movement raised the ante on the question of the relationship between democracy and efficiency:

> At the very heart of Progressivism was a basic conflict in social outlook. This conflict was between those whose hope for the future was primarily that of a planned and administered society, and those who, on the other hand, remained firm in the old liberal faith in an underlying harmony, which by natural and inevitable processes produces the greatest possible good if the necessary institutional and social reforms are made. (p. 17)

Waldo notes that in practice public administration theory has privileged administrative concerns at the expense of democratic values. Interpretations by a number of subsequent students of the Progressive reform era are consistent with Waldo's. Wiebe (1967), for example, has suggested that the Progressive "search for order" began with the moral notion of purifying the urban machine to "cure" democracy but evolved to a quest for enduring social harmony that depended on the effective efforts of an efficiently functioning bureaucracy. Skowronek (1982) sees the period as characterized by a merger between "the traditional interests of virtuous gentlemen in a politics of deference . . . [and] the new policy interests [of] the social scientist and the expert," which turned "ideological conflicts into matters of expertise" (pp. 44, 166). Haber's (1964) study of the turn-of-the-century cult of efficiency conceptualizes the tension as one between ignorance-as-evil and intelligence-as-good. Wilson (1887) himself, of course, couched the dynamic in terms of politics and administration, by means of the famous dichotomy. Administrators would serve democracy's interests by leaving politics to legislators and concentrating on the neutral, expert execution of legislative dictates.

In assessing the tension between democracy and efficiency in the history of public administration, Waldo (1948) sounded themes that evoke the images of expertise, leadership, and virtue that we have seen are pervasive in the modern administrative state. His review of what was known as the "Bureau movement," which promoted research into the workings of early-20th-century public agencies, summarizes these elements:

> The Bureau movement was a part of Progressivism, and its leaders were leaders of Progressivism. They were tired of the simple moralism of the nineteenth century, although paradoxically they were themselves fired with the moral fervor of humanitarianism and secularized Christianity. . . . They were sensitive to the appeals and promises of science, and put a simple trust in discovery of facts as the way of science and as a sufficient mode for solution of human problems. They accepted—they urged—the new positive conception of government, and verged upon the idea of a planned and managed society. They hated "bad" business, but found in business organization and procedure an acceptable prototype for public business. . . . They were ardent apostles of the "efficiency idea" and leaders in the movement for useful education. (pp. 32–33)

As the following discussion shows, morality, science, facts, positive government, business, leadership, and the efficiency idea were all notions shaped during the Progressive era by the thoughts and efforts of women, often by presenting an alternative to the mainstream understanding. These Progressive ideas cluster around the images reviewed in previous chapters, ideas that are still used to justify administrative authority: expertise (science, facts, business methods, efficiency), leadership (positive government, executive authority, education of citizens, intelligent cooperation), and virtue (morality). I suggest that women reformers played a significant role in establishing the terms and symbols by which proponents would promote and later defend positive administrative government but that women's interpretations of these terms and symbols fell into obscurity as the field developed during the 20th century. By restoring to light the part women played, I hope to call attention not only to their contributions per se but to the gender dilemmas and paradoxes that came to inhabit these key ideas as they were shaped during a crucial period in the development of the American administrative state.

The main points I want to make, based on historical literature, are these:

1. During the 19th century, a privatized understanding of virtue, one associated with ideas about "true womanhood," obscured the public significance of women's charitable activities.

2. Before the expansion of the administrative state, the central tension between democracy and efficiency was foreshadowed in the struggle of benevolent women to reconcile compassion for the needy with the increasing demand for businesslike methods in all areas of life.

3. Despite the perception of female benevolent work as an aspect of domesticity, it was actually the precursor of many current governmental service functions. When the need for government to take on a leading role in the delivery of services to the needy became apparent, women were in the forefront of efforts to secure the transfer.

4. Despite women's key role in developing services later assumed by the state and in promoting the need for governmental activism, the persistently feminine image of virtue (hence of reform as well) led proponents of the administrative state to couch their arguments in culturally masculine terms that have since obscured women's important role in the rise of public administration.[1]

True Womanhood

To understand the process and manner in which women influenced the development of the administrative state during the reform era, we must begin by considering how 19th-century ideas about gender roles affected shared understandings of public and private virtue and how, despite being restricted by convention to domestic virtue and private benevolence, women's charitable activities were inherently public in both location and significance.

I indicated in the previous chapter that the idea of republican motherhood during the Revolutionary period helped privatize understandings of virtue by making the home the chief site of virtue and women its principal champions. In the first half of the 19th century this idea expanded into what has been called the "cult of true womanhood" (Welter, 1976) or the "cult of domesticity" (Kraditor, 1968). Cott (1977) describes this cultural phenomenon as follows:

> Mother, father, and children grouped together in the private household ruled the transmission of culture, the maintenance of social stability, and the pursuit of happiness; the family's influence reached outward, underlying success or failure in church and state, and inward, creating individual character. . . . The emphasis placed on and agencies attributed to the family unit were new, and the importance given to women's roles as wives, mothers, and mistresses of households was unprecedented. The ministers, educators, and pious and educated women in the northern United States whose published writings principally documented this ethic made women's presence the essence of successful homes and families. Conversely, the "cult" both observed and prescribed specific behavior for women in the enactment of domestic life. (p. 2)

Cott points out that between 1780 and 1830 women's position in American society changed more profoundly than it had up to that time or would for the succeeding 50 years. The onset of industrialization, the spread of wage labor, and the consequent redefinition of work sharpened the distinctions between white men's and women's roles, a change reflected in the cult of domesticity. Whereas for black women and men, almost all of whom were slaves, no practical distinction between home and work was possible, white women of modest means entered the labor force as textile workers and primary-school teachers while those better off took on a variety of benevolent activities outside the home, such as visiting and caring for the sick and the poor, or threw themselves into causes including abolition, temperance, and women's rights.

Cott suggests that, although these new pursuits might seem to contradict reigning ideas about womanhood and domesticity, women's enlarged activities actually depended on this ideology: Because the cult of true womanhood allocated a separate sphere to middle- and upper-class white women and assigned them a vocation within it, it gave them a sense of their own identity that provided the strength to claim new roles (Cott, 1977, pp. 4–9, 200–201).

At the same time, Ginzberg (1990) has argued, because ideas of true womanhood, with their overtones of domesticity and private benevolence, hid from people of the time the public significance of women's public-interested work, limitations on their formal political participation were easier to maintain and perceptions about the femininity of virtue could persist. Such dynamics have helped obscure from historians of today—including those in public administration—the actual content of women's benevolent activities, their inherent publicness even while not formally associated with government, and their role as catalyst in the development of the positive state.

The centerpiece of the ideology of true womanhood was woman's moral superiority—her "piety, purity, submissiveness and domesticity" (Welter, 1976, p. 21), a premise that was used both to warrant woman's role as the moral guardian of home and society and to explain social phenomena such as the preponderance of males in prisons of the time (Ginzberg, 1990). The apparent gulf between woman's supposed moral excellence and the evils of society became the catalyst for the movement of women into social betterment activities: "The conviction that 'WOMAN,' as Sarah Hale put it [in 1855], was 'God's appointed agent of *morality*,' cemented the ideology of women's individual morality with the mandate to act to transform the world. . . . Women's agency was so gentle, pervasive, and unseen that the world would hardly know it was being subverted" (Ginzberg, 1990, pp. 14–15).

It is important to note that the idea of true womanhood was very much an elite white notion. Welter (1976) observes that women's benevolent work was supposed to be done out of pure affection and not for money or ambition: "'True feminine genius,' said [writer] Grace Greenwood, 'is ever timid, doubtful, and clingingly dependent; a perpetual childhood'" (p. 29). Obviously relatively few white women, and virtually no black women, could afford to work outside the home without thought of money, and "perpetual childhood," distasteful as it seems to us today, has a connotation of privilege and self-indulgence that requires a good bit of income to support. Lerner (1979) points out that the onset of industrialization led to increasing differences in the types of work done by different classes of women:

When female occupations, such as carding, spinning, and weaving, were transferred from home to factory, the poorer women followed their traditional work and became industrial workers. The women of the middle and upper classes . . . became ladies. . . . The images of "the lady" was elevated . . . [while] lower class women were simply ignored. (p. 25)

In addition, many white women were openly skeptical as to whether true womanhood was attainable by African American women even after emancipation. Freedwomen who sought to become homemakers were ridiculed as lazy instead of praised for their commitment to domesticity (Andolsen, 1986). Former masters and mistresses "would not agree to freedwomen 'playing the lady, being supported by their husbands like white folks'" (Sterling, 1984, p. xi). Race and class, therefore, limited participation in the cult of true womanhood to a relatively small proportion of women, whose comparatively privileged lives made them reluctant to find common cause with their less well-off sisters (Allen, 1983; Andolsen, 1986).

What did charitable women actually do? According to Ginzberg (1990), while women's benevolent organizations were generally separate from men's, this was not always the case, and—separate organizations or not—in actuality, women and men did virtually the same work, including fund-raising, teaching, visiting the needy, and administration. Women as well as men sat on committees, prepared reports and leaflets, wrote letters, organized meetings, lobbied for legislation, and sought appropriations for their organizations. Because most white women reformers were married to men of considerable means and influence, they relied on these connections in lobbying and in gaining appointments to committees and commissions. Lacking such connections, women of color had to content themselves with providing services privately (Gordon, 1990, p. 24). Thus, during a time when governments were little involved directly in what later came to be called social welfare, women were in the forefront of activity that set the stage for the moment when the need for the state to take the leading role would appear undeniable.

Ginzberg (1990) points out that women typically incorporated their charitable societies, a legal maneuver that enabled them to get around their own unequal status before the law (legally, married women were the wards of their husbands) and become, for practical purposes, legal "persons" who were not female. She suggests that "women's very interest in becoming incorporated challenges their insistence on a protected sphere" (p. 48). Incorporation also served to make women's benevolent activities appear more businesslike, an image that, as I discuss below, became increasingly important as the societal power of business corporations grew during the 19th century.

Men not only refrained from opposing women's charitable and reform activities but saw them as consistent with true womanhood, that is, with women's status as the inculcators of virtue. Because as nonvoters women were legally defined as outside the public sphere, men saw female benevolent work as "above politics" (Baker, 1990, p. 63). Women's benevolence was natural, even when it extended to the institutionalization of their work at first in private agencies, later in government itself. The mid- to late 19th century witnessed a growing assortment of such activities: "Besides the array of homes for wayward women, children, unemployed women, and destitute widows that sprouted up in antebellum cities, women increasingly founded industrial schools and houses of industry, establishments in which poor women earned wages in sewing and laundry rooms" (Ginzberg, 1990, p. 609). During and after the Civil War, women joined in government-sponsored relief work for soldiers and their families. For example, the Sanitary Commission, including its women's auxiliaries, provided food, clothing, and nurses for the war effort, and women allied themselves with state boards of charity that proliferated after the war to coordinate relief activities (Ginzberg, 1990, pp. 134, 196–197). In the latter part of the 19th century, white women's clubs established libraries and girls' trade schools, sponsored legislation to get rid of sweat shops and make tenements safer, pressed for a juvenile court system, and helped instigate measures for clean water and sewage disposal.

Black women, of course, were barred from membership in "Progressive" circles (Neverdon-Morton, 1989). Their own clubs, set up at first to defend black men against lynching, soon expanded into a wide range of activities: forming kindergartens, nursery schools, day-care programs, orphanages and old folks' homes, and in general trying to make up for the lack of such institutions in or available to the black community, particularly in the South (Brooks-Higginbotham, 1993; Giddings, 1985; Lerner, 1979).[2]

Despite the many spheres into which it extended and the important societal changes it wrought, however, women's charitable activity produced little change in widespread beliefs about their proper role. Their benevolence was still seen as private and an expression of domestic rather than citizen-like virtue.

Becoming Businesslike

Although women's philanthropic activity began as an expression and symbol of feminine virtue, over the course of the 19th century it had to reshape itself in response to cultural developments. One was the growth of social science and the increasing emphasis place on "facts" as the necessary basis not only for effective benevolent action but for the amelioration of social conditions of all sorts. It appears from historical studies that in some quarters the commitment to social science was seen as harmonious with women's interest and participation in betterment activities; in fact, social science was perceived to be part of women's proper sphere. In 1874, Franklin Sanborn, secretary of the American Social Science Association, said that "the work of social science is literally women's work . . . but there is room for all sexes and ages" (quoted in Leach, 1980, p. 292). He referred to social science as the feminine side of political economy. Women could incorporate the concerns and methods of social science in their work because neither they nor men seemed to see them as inconsistent with benevolence based on moral sentiments.

Gradually, however, the feminine science of benevolent work took on increasingly masculine flavor that was at odds with women's existing habits of the heart. For example, Louisa Lee Schuyler, founder of New York State's Charities Aid Association, commented, "The efficiency of all associated effort depends largely upon good organization, the enforcement of discipline and the thoroughness of the work." Schuyler emphasized "obedience to rules," "esprit de corps," and other "soldierly qualities" (quoted in Ginzberg, 1990, p. 193), invoking norms the Civil War had made compelling but that also blended well with the scientific concerns for order and proper procedure. Ginzberg (1990) observes that the demands of relief work during the war proved a watershed for benevolent activity, weakening earlier hopes of moral perfection, pointing up the need for systematic volunteer efforts, and replacing feminine sentiment with realistic, "manly exertion." Postwar philanthropy paid increasing homage to the more masculine values such as efficiency and science (pp. 133–134), gradually coming to see systematic methods as ends in themselves rather than as instrumental to benevolence.

Over the course of the 19th century, two paradoxical developments stand out: Within the arena of charitable work itself, the institutionalization, corporatization, and professionalization of benevolent activities gradually suppressed the idea that women had anything unique (that is, moral sentiment) to bring to such pursuits; however, at the same time in society at large, reform work as a whole came increasingly to be seen as feminine and ineffective, particularly when contrasted with the vigorous masculinity of ballot-box politics. On the one hand, the increasingly businesslike approach to charity work demanded professional standards; from this perspective, it was the absence of femininity—of softheartedness, of emotionality—that made a particular woman an effective charity worker. As Ginzberg (1990) notes, this denial of differences in style and circumstance between men and women both obscured real power differentials between the sexes and barred the development of radical insights that might have led to a reduction in sexual inequality.

On the other hand, in the wider world the perception of virtue as a feminine (therefore soft and sentimental) characteristic reinforced the distinction between real—that is, partisan—politics and the nonpartisan reform movement. Party politics was a kind of rough-and-tumble white male club, a defining characteristic of masculinity. Metaphors of warfare, cockfighting, and boxing abounded: "Editors derided opponents as 'grandmas' and 'eunuchs.' Campaign speakers found themselves dismissed as feeble, weak, and shrill" (Edwards, 1997, p. 15). Party stalwarts disparaged male reformers as politically impotent, calling them "namby-pamby, goody-goody gentlemen" who "sip cold tea," "political hermaphrodites," "the third sex of politics," "Miss Nancys," and "man milliners." As Hofstadter (1963, pp. 188–190) notes, "To be active in politics was a man's business, whereas to be engaged in reform movements meant constant association with aggressive, reforming, moralizing women"—clearly not a happy prospect. From the party man's perspective, the effort to remove any aspect of government—for example, public administration—from politics seemed an effort to weaken, even to render impotent, the manly vigor of citizenship; similarly, the campaign for female suffrage threatened to wipe out an important distinction between women and men: "If women voted, they would abandon the home and womanly virtues; men would lose their manhood and women would begin to act like men" (Baker, 1990, p. 69). Thus, in this instance as elsewhere, gender dynamics wrought a paradox that, regardless of the angle from which it is viewed, helped maintain distinctions that worked to women's disadvantage. Where their perspectives and efforts had shaped an entire sphere of public-interested work (the sphere of benevolence), women's contributions came to be obscured by a rhetoric of professionalism that, as it denigrated moral feeling, rejected any difference in women's and men's approaches; on the other hand, in that arena of public life from which women were most firmly barred (electoral politics), a rhetoric of difference hindered women's attainment of full citizenship and preserved the notion of real politics as a matter of tough-minded masculinity.

I have suggested that as women's benevolent work proliferated, the preferred approach became increasingly businesslike, a tendency that worked to obliterate any perceived value in the uniqueness of women's contributions. In fact, this encounter between women's benevolent activities and the dictates of efficiency and science is a harbinger of the tension between democracy and efficiency that Waldo (1948) sees at the heart of public administration theory. In the development of public administration, Waldo argues, efforts to "harmonize" the two sets of values generally ended in efficiency taking precedence over democracy, particularly by insisting that there was really no quarrel between them. Facts would show the way, and among persons of intelligence in possession of facts there could be no serious disagreement about what to do. For example, Allen's (1907) *Efficiency Democracy* declared, "Without . . . facts upon which to base judgment, the public cannot intelligently direct and control the administration of township, county, city, state, or nation. Without intelligent control by the public, no efficient, progressive, triumphant democracy is possible" (p. ix). But a similar clash had already occurred. In the case of women's public-spirited work, a set of moral values—the desire to help, to improve, to change society—came up against demands for objectivity, efficiency, and science and began to be absorbed by them. For example, at the Association for Improving the Conditions of the Poor, a pioneer in what became known as "scientific charity," female caseworkers had to follow an established protocol for determining which families in need to visit and how often. "After learning that they could not keep an orderly [note]pad and do disorderly work, and that the little feminine devices to keep up appearances would be quickly disclosed to the questioning supervisor, they . . . began seriously to take advantage of the savings that came from the system" (Allen, 1907, pp. 162–164). The need to be scientific and businesslike in order to appear competent could not be gainsaid. Benevolent work had to be systematic and professionalized in order to be effective and to justify the expense and effort devoted to it. Indeed, if the home itself could be seen as a "factory of citizenship" (Haber, 1964, p. 62), it would appear that the positive aspects of women's differences from men—those that could justify room in the public sphere for their charitable work—were in danger of being supplanted entirely in the public consciousness by those differences that were used to justify restrictions on women's social roles. Thus women could and did continue to play an important part in advancing reform causes but under a rubric of social scientific efficiency that obscured the nature of their contributions. At the same time, public administration was developing during a period when benevolent and reform work were increasingly perceived as feminine in contrast to the vigor of party politics, a paradox that led male reformers to try to purge the new science of public administration of any taint of sentimentality—of femininity—by making sure that it was businesslike.

Shaping the Administrative State

From the tension between benevolence and expertise in the wider sphere of charitable and reform work, I now turn to the part that women played specifically in the rise of the administrative state. The roots of the nascent administrative state in women's compassionate work with the needy and their more general interest in curing urban ills have been obscured partly due to a general tendency among historians to overlook women's contributions but also because the feminine image of charitable work has hidden from later observers its public implications. I suggest that women's efforts to perpetuate and institutionalize their philanthropic activity, along with the perceptions they had about its social meaning, directly influenced the rise of the administrative state during the Progressive era. In a time when reformers as a group came increasingly to advocate that government play a leadership role in societal betterment, women reformers were in the vanguard, seeking to sustain forms of businesslike benevolence by securing government sponsorship of them. Because women saw the growing need for what we now think of as social services, a need whose scope they realized could only be handled by government, they deliberately sought both new policies and the administrative capacity to carry them forward. Thus women were notably responsible for the ways in which threads of competence, virtue, and governmental leadership came together in the late 19th and early 20th centuries to launch a major rationale for the administrative state.

Well-to-do white women, largely excluded from men's reform clubs, formed their own organizations and attacked a wide range of urban problems, while social welfare reformers, predominantly women, founded settlement houses in city neighborhoods inhabited mostly by poor immigrants. Instead of concentrating on the structures and administrative processes of municipal governments, as male municipal reformers did, clubwomen and settlement residents aimed their efforts directly at living conditions in cities. Clubwomen and women of the settlement houses typically attacked the problems of cities in what they thought of as women's ways, calling their activities "municipal housekeeping." They justified their involvement in city problems as an aspect of true womanhood, arguing that protection of society's virtue made it necessary for them to work outside as well as inside the home.

Many of the women's clubs initially concentrated on neighborhood cleanup and beautification campaigns, but they soon extended their idea of municipal housekeeping to broader aspects of civic affairs. They saw that

> municipal organization had to do with things it was essential should be well done if their efforts as mothers were not to be negatived. The water pumped to their houses, the street, the alley, the school, the hospital, the street car, the park, are all powerful aids to the development of a healthy and enlightened family life, if they are well managed; but they are also agencies for evil, if poorly managed. (Deardorff, 1914, p. 72)

As their perspective broadened, reform women became involved in campaigns for better sanitation, garbage collection, medical inspection of children, the treatment of juvenile offenders, child labor, and working conditions in factories. They advocated legislation or increased appropriations for civic improvements, sometimes even running for local office themselves, where this was possible. As Mary Ritter Beard (1915) put it, "In years gone by, women would have stood by the tub or faucet and thanked bountiful providence for water of any amount or description; but now, as they stand there, their minds reach out through the long chain of circumstances that connect the faucet and tub with the gentlemen who sit in aldermanic conclave" (p. 206). Clubwomen argued that they played a special part in public life, namely, "the power to make, of any place in which [they] may happen to live, a home for all who come there" (Bowlker, 1912, p. 863).

Settlement house residents pioneered a number of programs that subsequently were taken over by municipal governments, including playgrounds, the first juvenile court, the first state employment bureau, health and sanitation inspection, special education, children's clinics, and housing inspection. In 1906, Mary Simkhovitch of College Settlement in New York reported, "In large cities, one settlement activity after another has been taken over by city government—training, kindergartens, playgrounds; public school functions; departments of health and of parks have expanded" (p. 568). By 1914, George McAneny, president of the New York City Board of Aldermen, could say, "There is hardly a function of the settlement twenty years ago that has not passed into the hands of progressive city governments today. The settlement will always show the way, for it and the social worker represent the advance line of our progress" ("Settlement Pioneers," 1914, p. 638). Like clubwomen, settlement leaders often used metaphors of home and family and of friendship and hospitality to characterize their activity. They recognized the importance of sound administration of municipal activities, but they tended to interpret effectiveness not solely in terms of efficiency. Sophonisba Breckinridge, a Hull House resident and pioneer in social work education, wrote in one of her textbooks that economy and efficiency meant something different "in their application to public welfare" than they did in business and industry: "In the latter fields the profit-seeking impulse makes the balance sheet the final criterion. In political and domestic organization, human well-being under conditions of justice, freedom, and equality, are the objects sought, and business administration can never be the guide to truly successful organization" (Breckinridge, 1927, pp. 366–367). Thus women's social welfare reform work centered around the distinctiveness of women's role in society and the perceptions and sensitivities that women, as a result of their life experience, could bring to municipal reform. Over time, however, justifications based on distinctiveness lost ground, particularly after women won the vote in 1920. With the franchise, they had won legal equality, or so it seemed, and social advocacy based on their "different" viewpoints was far less compelling than it had once been.

The Gender of Reform

Because public administration as a conscious enterprise developed during a time when virtue was seen as a feminine quality, male Progressives felt a need to make reform appear more muscular. Accused of being sissies by people they thought of as party hacks and rascals, the men of public administration responded by attempting to purge reform of any taint of sentimentality—of femininity—by making sure that it was seen as tough-minded, rational, scientific, and businesslike. Leaders of the New York Bureau of Municipal Research, a pioneering reform organization that sponsored the first professional training for careers in public administration, consistently emphasized the scientific and business-oriented nature of its work. Both science and business were linked with masculinity at the time. Male reformers hoped to turn aside insinuations about their deficient manhood by clothing their activities in masculine garb—science, efficiency, and executive command and control. The image of the man of science "cleaving the Gordian knot of politics with one swift blow" (Haber, 1964, p. 59) was common around the turn of the century; "science" suggested disinterestedness and rigor, and "management" was allied with ideas of mastery, firm guidance, and constraint. According to Frederick Cleveland (1913), a leader of the New York Bureau, the best thing about the municipal research movement, which grounded itself in science, was its "virility" (p. 103). The bureau men insisted that they were not "volunteers" in the ordinary sense but expert scientists. Volunteers were people who acted on the basis of emotions rather than reason; by extension, volunteers were amateurs rather than professionals armed with scientific knowledge.

The gender implications of the distinction between the volunteer and the professional were clear to reformers of both sexes. In 1912, Henry Bruere of the New York Bureau exclaimed, "So long as government remains inefficient, volunteer and detached effort to remove social handicaps will continue a hopeless task" (p. 100). William Allen, another Bureau leader, contrasted the Bureau's scientific fact-finding with the worthy but small-scale efforts of the settlement houses, where residents were providing "three shower baths" instead of working to set up a municipal bathhouse capable of handling "9,000 tenement residents a day," or teaching English to "a dozen Swedish maids" instead of doing something about "200,000 children behind in their school grade" (Allen, 1907, p. 274). Bureau leader Charles A. Beard summed up the scientific approach as "a contribution to the processes by which modern mankind is striving with all its resources to emancipate itself from the tyranny of rules of thumb and the blind regimen of nature, becoming conscious of its destiny as an all-conquering power" (quoted in Waldo, 1948, p. 33n.).

In contrast, settlement leaders conceived of public administration as a practice the effectiveness of which required sensitivity to human feeling.

In her early investigation of Cook County's outdoor relief office, Julia Lathrop reported,

> The methods of this office, with its records kept as each changing administration chooses, its dole subject to every sort of small political influence, and its failure to co-operate with private charities, are not such as science can approve.... We are shocked by the crudeness of the management which huddles men, women, and children, the victims of misfortune and the relics of dissipation, the idle, the ineffective criminal, the penniless convalescent, under one roof and one discipline. (quoted in Addams, 1935, p. 302)

According to Jane Addams, the county relief agency was so fearful that outdoor relief would expand endlessly that needy couples forced to go to the poorhouse were separated into men's and women's units and allowed to talk to one another only once a week, and then with heavy screening between them. "Such a state of mind," Addams (1935) commented, "affords one more example of the danger of administering any human situation upon theory uncorrected by constant experience" (pp. 70–71). Settlement residents were particularly sensitive to the human impact of public institutional practices because in their neighborhoods they frequently encountered men and women being treated as cases subject to rigid administrative procedures instead of as human beings. As a result, their theories of public administration aimed to combine empathy with efficiency; both, they argued, were necessary ingredients of effectiveness.

Conclusion

In this chapter I suggested that our understanding of the development of the administrative state in thought and deed during the Progressive era is inadequate without awareness of the gender paradoxes that lie beneath the stories we ordinarily tell. We have seen that women's benevolent work was public both in its performance and its significance. Far from restricting themselves to wifely duties, both white and African American women were notable presences in charitable activity. Over time, this work led both women and men to see the need to expand the responsibilities of governments and those who could to work actively to stimulate governmental involvement. The tasks that reformers sought to turn over to government had largely been considered women's work and seen as grounded in a peculiarly feminine virtue. As women's philanthropic work merged with the municipal reform effort, male reformers perceived the need to remove the taint of femininity that haunted reform (particularly in contrast to the muscular vigor of party politics) by ensuring that it was seen as businesslike and efficient—tough rather than sentimental. As long as social betterment was virtue personified and the persona was Woman, it could be seen (despite obvious evidence to the contrary) as private. Because the worlds of both business and government were traditionally male, to make good works efficient by turning them over to reformed public administration was to make them masculine. The original rhetoric of difference (true womanhood) that had made women's benevolent work possible in the first place now had to be suppressed in favor of a rhetoric of professionalism and efficiency, large powers, and the harnessing of forces; after women won the franchise in 1920, the rhetoric of difference virtually disappeared. In the process, women's central place in an entire cultural-political phenomenon, the reform movement out of which self-conscious public administration emerged, was obliterated. Yet the tension between democracy and efficiency, between participation and professionalism, between values and facts, around which so much of the conversation in contemporary public administration revolves, shaped and was shaped by women's role in reform. The idea that the need for good management limits the feasibility of democracy in administration is essentially the same argument as the one that reform women bowed to, namely that benevolence had to become businesslike to survive.

Among the lessons of this excursion into reform era history are the unobserved gender dimensions of public administration's formative processes: how what we have thought of as neutral ideas like efficiency, businesslike methods, and the science of administration include problematic gender biases that are reflected in their historical development. Until we focus our attention on these matters, our justifications of administrative governance will continue to present women with insoluble dilemmas. Women do not simply represent "redecoration" of the house of public administration nor will they (we) be content to serve in this capacity. On the contrary, the project is not simply one of refurbishment but of reconstruction from the ground(s) up.

Notes

1. For an extended discussion of the role of women in municipal government reform and in the development of the field of public administration, see Stivers (2000a), an important source for the balance of this chapter.

2. The lives of 19th-century African American women led them to see gender dynamics of the time in somewhat more trenchant terms than were apparently possible for even the most ardent white women reformers. As Carby (1986) notes, Anna Julia Cooper argued that white men's imperialist impulses were nurtured at home by white women preoccupied with maintaining their own economic privilege. Ida B. Wells maintained that the exalted moral status of white women served as the basis for a campaign of fear and intimidation against black men that persisted for the better part of a century. White southerners gained northern tolerance of lynching by characterizing it as a response to the rape of white women by black men; Wells argued that the basis for this concession on the part of white northern men was their sense of ownership over white women's bodies. Carby observes that Wells's "analysis of lynching provided for a . . . detailed dissection of patriarchal power . . . showing how it could manipulate sexual ideologies to justify political and economic subordination. . . . Wells was able to demonstrate how a patriarchal system . . . used its control over women to attempt to completely circumscribe the actions of black males" (p. 309).

7

Paths Toward Change

Defending the American administrative state has always been a precarious enterprise because of endemic popular suspicions about bureaucracy (see King, Stivers, & Collaborators, 1998). Now that we have considered the gender dilemmas in these arguments, however, they seem even more problematic than has been generally apparent. Into the prevailing debate over the rightful basis of administrative discretion this book has introduced considerations such as these: the match between widespread ideas about masculinity and norms of professionalism, leadership, and management; the extent to which bureaucratic structures and procedures, administrative career patterns, and the dynamics of public organizational life depend on women's disproportionate responsibility for domestic work; the administrative state's part in sustaining gender roles that limit women's life choices; and the suppressed femininity of important administrative canons like responsiveness, service, and benevolence. I have argued that the self-understanding of public administration, as reflected in its images of leadership and management, expertise, and virtue, is culturally masculine (although its masculinity is as yet unacknowledged) but that it also reflects a significant element of femininity (although consciousness of its femininity has yet to dawn).

I have suggested that the masculinity of public administrative theory privileges men and their interests by establishing boundaries on thought and action that exclude from positions of authority all but a relatively few "exceptional" women. The argument has pointed to conceptual dichotomies such as public/private and efficiency/democracy that not only work against the existing interests and needs of women but that cannot be sustained when we examine actual practices. I have criticized the tendency in public administrative thought toward heedless universalizing, by means of which historically male practices and ideas are made to stand for humanity as a whole without any examination of their possible limitations where women are concerned. The discussion has also claimed that public administration theories emerge from and reinforce material realities that oppress women. These realities include the double burden of housework and paid employment that working women bear, their disproportionate relegation to the lower bureaucratic ranks, the glass ceiling that blocks their access to the positions of greatest power and monetary reward, and their lack of fit with organizational expectations about professional and managerial behavior.

In this final chapter, I want to consider some of the implications of these gaps and paradoxes in public administration theory. My working assumption is that unease over public criticism of the bureaucracy will not dissipate simply by fretting over public administration's negative images in the eyes of the general public, any more than women have advanced their own liberation just by worrying about being seen as emotional, irrational, or passive. What we really ought to be doing, in thinking about public administration, is examining our simultaneous dependence on and denial of gender dichotomies. My belief is that only by exploring public administration's gender dilemmas, instead of denying their existence or minimizing their significance, will we begin to develop a form of public administration that merits public approbation. Only then will we find paths that lead us toward change.

Toward a Feminist Theory of Public Administration

Because feminist theorizing is somewhat like trying to think in a language that does not yet exist, that cannot exist as long as historically masculine experiences and values are taken as "human," outlining the substance of a feminist theory of public administration is a matter of catching glimpses of what might be rather than setting forth a full-blown vision. As French feminist Julia Kristeva observes, political reality makes it necessary to struggle in the name of women even as we acknowledge that under current circumstances a woman can exist only as her refusal of that which is given: "I therefore understand by 'woman' . . . that which cannot be represented, that which is not spoken, that which remains outside naming and ideologies" (quoted in Moi, 1985, p. 163). A feminist theory of public administration, as something that *must* be even though it cannot yet be, begins by identifying the small points of entry through which considerations of gender have infiltrated existing theory simply because of its dependence, in order to be coherent, on saying what it is not. As Johnson (1987) puts it, womanhood is the "uncanny alien always already in the house"; the relationship between the alien and the master of the house (between woman and man) is that "each is already inhabited by the other as a difference from itself" (p. 35). In this sense, public administration does indeed have vulnerable aspects, and I have tried to identify some of them in this book: elements in defenses of public administration that reflect gender paradoxes and contradictions, and threads (threats?) of womanhood that run through the history and current practice of public administration. I have argued that public administration at once depends on and denies the existence of womanhood—both the life circumstances of actual women and the unacknowledged gender dimensions of concepts like professionalism, leadership, virtue, and service. What of the paths toward change?

Over the past decade, a number of aspects of public administration have come in for examination from perspectives that could reasonably be called feminist. For example, Morton and Lindquist (1997) took a fresh look at Mary Parker Follett, asking whether her work could fairly be characterized as feminist. They see parallels between Follett and feminism in (a) Follett's relational view of reality; (b) Follett's idea of knowledge, which is grounded in experience and recognizes the effects of power; and (c) Follett's ethical idea of "integration," which closely matches feminist emphasis on people's needs over abstract principles. Morton and Lindquist conclude that Follett's work "offers an important example of how women's practical experiences, or the feminist perspective, may be effectively incorporated into theories of democratic governance and administration" (p. 366). My own examination of Follett suggests that her work has been unjustly neglected because her ideas, which are culturally "feminine," do not fit the masculine world of management. This is most clearly seen in her implicit rejection of organizational hierarchy (Stivers, 1996a). Follett (1924) argued, in contrast to virtually every management thinker from Chester Barnard on, that organizational purpose comes out of organizational process, rather than being imposed from above: "The purpose in front will always mislead us. Psychology now gives us end as moment in process" (p. 81). Few more fundamental challenges to conventional management thinking have ever been posed. Given the masculinity of management thinking, with its emphasis on control, it is not surprising that this aspect of Follett's thought, despite its centrality, has been widely ignored in favor of less controversial statements that seem to hold promise for improving productivity or reducing class warfare between labor and management.

☞ Unfortunately, relatively little progress toward a feminist theory of public administration can be made by reassessing the classic work of women theorists, since Follett stands virtually alone in this category. Considerable work can be and has been done, however, in rethinking many of the field's central theoretical concepts. Several efforts have been made, for example, to reexamine the concept of rationality from a feminist perspective. The rationality of public administration, as we have seen, has been pivotal in thinking about the nature of bureaucracy, about the character of bureaucratic thinking, about the appropriateness of a norm of professionalism in public service, and about the fit basis for policy decisions. Hendricks (1992) has argued from a feminist standpoint for the inclusion of a "woman-centered" perspective in public administration, which begins with "de-centering" the male standard, particularly with respect to rational legalism. Instead of treating women "like men," Hendricks recommends that laws and regulations deal with women as "persons by self-definition and on their own terms," and that they acknowledge an existing power differential between women and men. Schreurs (2000) has analyzed rationality in the Anglo-American discourse on public organization. She finds that instrumental rationality dominates scholarship in this arena, that is, an interpretation of rationality based on means-ends calculation and on efficiency. Schreurs calls for a broader repertoire of interpretive strategies than the conventional model exemplified in the work of Max Weber and Herbert Simon, a menu of strategies that would include critical theory, feminist theory, and postmodernism.

Based on a comprehensive review of the various defenses of the legitimacy of administrative power, McSwite (1997) has found that the image of the Man of Reason is central to the entire enterprise of justification. For McSwite, the very term "reason" in the theoretical conversation stands for the capacity to judge or exercise discretion. Men of Reason recognize that neither science nor a commitment to moral principles will be sufficient to identify the right thing to do in any given situation. They acknowledge the importance of science and ethics and support their use; the key axiom that forms the basis for their ethos is "submission to objective reality." But human minds are incapable of grasping the elements of this reality in an ultimately reliable way; therefore, Men of Reason argue, we need people among us "who try the hardest to think, feel, and live in a way that moves them as close as possible to Truth and Good. The rest of us let our own idiosyncratic concerns shape our thoughts and feelings. . . . Respect for science and moral theory is essential for keeping things in their place and minimizing the dissonance with which Men of Reason have to cope. People must be held in the place of followers and Men of Reason in the place of leaders" (pp. 233–234). The Man of Reason resolves the ambiguity that cannot be gotten rid of through science or ethical principles by means of his individual discretion: "In the final analysis, he decides alone" (p. 235).

McSwite argues that in practice the Man of Reason can be either male or female. The gendered basis of reason comes from its fundamental reliance on boundedness—we know we are behaving rationally if we can specify our terms, what they encompass and what they do not—and its inability to deal with any elements that cannot be so specified. McSwite argues that, symbolically, "Woman" stands for that which cannot be brought within the boundaries of language (compare Kristeva's comment earlier in this section that "woman" stands for what remains outside naming and ideologies). If this is the case, no strategy based on making public administration more rational or reasonable will move it beyond gender. According to McSwite, we have to turn instead to something other than rules for bounding concepts in the hope of accessing objective reality; we have to turn to making a world "by developing the kinds of relationships with each other that allow us to figure out what we want to do next" (p. 261). Our collaboration in actual situations will be the basis from which together we make our world meaningful.

As the McSwite argument suggests, not all the analyses a feminist would want to encourage are overtly feminist. Many advance feminist aims by reconsidering key concepts in a manner that questions gender assumptions implicitly. For example, consider Dudley's (1996) examination of an Office of Management and Budget circular defining governmental functions as those that require "either the exercise of discretion in applying governmental authority or the use of value judgments in making decisions for the government" (p. 73). Dudley argues that the boundaries between public, commercial, and nonprofit sectors are fluid enough in practice that it is impossible to set a rule for defining "governmental" that will establish its autonomy once and for all, such as by reference to such ideas as sovereignty, control over property, or authority to use force. Instead, Dudley offers the idea of the "situated self . . . a self defined through connection" (p. 84). In other words, what is governmental will emerge by means of a larger political dialogue in particular situations across sectors. As in the McSwite (1997) argument but without explicit reference to gender, this argument rejects reliance on the establishment of firm conceptual boundaries or decision rules and accepts the need to work through the meaning of terms like "governmental" in reference to particular situations and with the inclusion of diverse perspectives. The turn away from reliance on concepts such as power and authority and toward the idea of a situated self is consistent with many feminist arguments, even though not so labeled.

Given the negative connotation of "feminist" among many people in the field, both men and women, it seems important to point to and encourage discussions such as Dudley's, whose orientation and persuasive strategies destabilize central gendered concepts in the field without being explicitly based on feminist theory. Another example of such a reconsideration is my reflection on the idea of responsiveness, a concept that has been denigrated at least in part because of its femininity (Stivers, 1994). I suggested that our idea of responsiveness not be limited by the notion that being responsive to citizens is somehow necessarily biased or corrupt. Instead, administrators might think of responsiveness as a positive skill captured in the idea of listening, a skill that opens administrative practice to the perspectives of others outside it in order to "glean important information, define situations more carefully, hear neglected aspects and interests, and facilitate just and prudent action in often turbulent environments" (Stivers, 1994, p. 368). Given the association of responsiveness with femininity, such an argument at least implicitly aims at moving toward a more gender-balanced image of the public administrator.

New Images in Public Administration

Let us reconsider some of the paradoxical concepts raised in earlier chapters to discover neglected dimensions, reflection on which might bear fruit.

Expertise

We saw that current ideas about bureaucratic competence stress a neutral objectivity that depends on a separated self mastering nature and sees the ideal form of knowledge as hard data; this sort of objectivity supports the individual liberty valued in liberal philosophy by making the state a neutral arbiter among competing claims. The feminist perspective, however, reveals this model of knowledge to be anything but neutral because of the centuries-old association between nature and woman and because the liberal state depends on the subordination of women. I argued that forms of neutrality like the Brownlow Report's passion for anonymity or the Blacksburg Manifesto's agency perspective depend heavily on the ability of the individual administrator to identify with the constructed filigree of interpreted values, practices, and perceptions that comprise a particular agency, which are a function of its history and prior membership. Dependence on the compatibility between agency perspective and individual identity puts a premium on similarities of life experience, including those rooted in gender, race, and class, that poses a dilemma for women and others who are different from the agency norm.

On a theoretical level, a feminist interpretation of the agency perspective would entail first acknowledging the partiality of what has been considered universal; in other words, feminism would argue for developing a sociology of agency knowledge and values in which gender, race, and class are major considerations. Such a move would dispel the notion that the agency perspective takes shape in a cultural vacuum. An agency cannot be sure of its ability to ascertain the "widest possible interpretation of the public interest" called for by the Blacksburg Manifesto if its judgments are circumscribed by the values and experiences of a relatively narrow range of humanity. Nor can theorists argue confidently for the legitimacy of agency interpretations of the public interest without exploring how to transform limited perspectives into ones that truly take diverse points of view into account. On a practical level, continuing efforts to diversify agency staffs through affirmative action and pay equity policies will support a diversity-based public interest but not unless the agency culture is such that all agency members are both unafraid to bring to bear their own life experiences and values on agency thinking and committed to a group process that will transform individual perspectives into something that is both diverse and universal and thus can be justified as the public interest. Confronted with race and gender diversity in their membership, institutions, including public agencies, have a way of trusting the universality of established values and practices while seeing as biased the new ideas injected as the result of an increasingly diverse workforce. (The establishment hue and cry over "political correctness" is exactly this sort of reaction, an effort to position the views and proposals of minorities and women as somehow biased, whereas the conventional wisdom and accepted canon are not.) Lowering barriers to people who were previously discriminated against means having to lower barriers to the possibility that their ideas will result in real changes in business as usual.

Images of objectivity and autonomy not only separate the individual from the field but also raise the administrator above the field. Professional competence reduces those over whom authority is exercised to a state of dependence: Expertise depoliticizes the claims of clients, discounts the values of citizens' views, and dissociates itself from nonprofessional workers. From the feminist perspective, we need a form of competence that is non-hierarchical: professionals who rather than seeing their own knowledge as preeminent believe that all parties to the situation at hand—clients, citizens, other workers—have perspectives that are necessary parts of the whole, without which the widest possible public interest cannot be ascertained.

To take this line of thinking one step further, the notion of science that underlies professionalism has a historical and conceptual gender bias. As Noble (1992) has shown, "Western science evolved only half human, in a world without women" (p. xiii). Rooted in the struggle of Latin Christendom to establish itself as the source of orthodoxy, the culture of Western science grew out of the identification of religious heresy with women and the parallel exclusion of women from universities established under church auspices. Within this culture, down to the present day, femininity is an aberration. The establishment of the field of public administration during the Progressive era took place on the basis that "science" would provide the key to improving government agencies—thus the field's founding has decidedly masculine roots. Despite this, however, female reformers of the time developed their own understanding of science, one centered not around objectivity and rigor but around connectedness (Stivers, 2000a). Settlement leaders operated on the premise that "only that which is lived can be understood and translated to others" (Simkhovitch, 1938, p. 39). Trustworthy, accurate knowledge came from "minute familiarity"; science, in fact, "demanded" not only alertness but also the kind of sympathy that came from intimate knowledge of problem situations. "Scientific disinterestedness [called] for, not the separatedness of the

observer, but suspended judgment in the midst of action" (Woods &
Kennedy, 1922/1970, p. 59). Facts were arrived at by means of connection
with the field of study rather than an investigative posture of objectivity.

The perspective of women reformers suggests the possibility that a
new understanding of science and professionalism is possible for public
administration. Such an understanding would reject both rigid objectivity and untrammeled bias. Science would be a practice not divorced from
life but immersed in it. Public administrators would be not experts raised
above the people, setting the terms by which public life would be defined
and understood, but neighbors. Studying public problems would involve
as collaborators those whose lived experience makes them experts on the
situations at hand. Public administration would constitute a "community
of practical scholars" (Woods, 1906, p. 475) dedicated to the application
of pragmatic knowledge to the great issues of the day, a science that grap-
ples with situations instead of observing them from a distance, working
to humanize the processes of government in order to meet human needs,
and collaborating with citizens in developing usable knowledge.

Continued insistence on conventional science as a guiding principle
for public administration may have the long-term effect of destabilizing
the tension between efficiency and democracy in a way that has negative
consequences. Efficiency questions are assumed to have right answers: If
only we can do the calculations right, we can come up with the most efficient (least cost, or most cost-effective) way to accomplish a given objective. But as many political theorists have argued, the defining characteristic
of political questions—such as what constitutes "democracy" in a given
situation—is that they do not have right answers in the scientific sense.
They are questions we can and do continue to argue about even as we may
adopt a working definition in a particular case. The fact that such questions can never be settled once and for all is what makes them political. If
so, insistence on finding "objective" (scientifically generated) answers to
administrative questions implies that such questions have no political
dimensions. Maintaining the tension between efficiency and democracy
(or administration and politics) means "refusing to get it right" (Stivers,
1996b), that is, giving up the quest for once-and-for-all answers in favor
of participatory processes such as those settlement leaders developed,
where the knowledge process itself is collaborative and democratic.

One additional revision is needed in our image of professional competence. It must move beyond the myth of the heroic male professional
who sacrifices "selfish" family concerns in single-minded fashion to his

career. The difficulty is not only that most women find it difficult or impossible to live up to such an ideal but that the ideal itself is warped, in that it compartmentalizes life and the men and women who live it, relegating the family to a lesser status and performance of its responsibilities to lesser people. From the feminist perspective, the legitimate public administrator will be a whole person, one who is understood to have developed in and to be a continuing member of a family; the work of agencies will be seen as supporting and supported by the wider dimensions of its members' lives, and agency personnel policies will reflect this understanding. Policies such as parental leave and on-site day-care facilities will be seen (just as public schools are seen) as in the public interest because they promote the nurturing and development of children; they will not be viewed merely as meeting the needs of individual employees.

Leadership

In reviewing ideas and images of leadership in public administration, I argued that, in light of the lack of research evidence linking it with organizational outcomes, leadership should be considered an ideology that rationalizes (among other power relations) existing role expectations based on gender, race and class. Cultural ideas about leadership match notions of white professional male behavior and serve as a filter to keep most people who do not conform to these expectations from becoming leaders.

Images of leadership are questionable from a feminist perspective. We saw, for example, that just as the operation of vision distances the one who looks from the objects in view, the visionary leader objectifies and—particularly in the guise of "manager"—asserts control over others in the organizational situation. In the image of the leader as decision maker, emphases on taking charge, being task oriented, exerting authority, and maximizing rational efficiency all suggest that people "need" to be led and that participatory process is purely an instrument in the achievement of organizational goals, if not a ritual acknowledgment of the "human factor" that stubbornly refuses to subsume itself under the dictates of management. Images of the inspirational or symbolic leader are based on the assumption that, regardless of their own self-identities, people find it equally easy to identify with or emulate warriors and father figures. Because of the cultural masculinity of these images of leadership and management, and because in actual fact most leader-managers are men, women who move into these positions encounter the problem of whether to display characteristics that will mark them as inappropriately masculine or strive for a softer image and risk being seen as indecisive. Thus, women are faced with the task of managing their gender, a problem male leaders do not have to try to solve.

From a feminist perspective, one obvious solution to the dilemma with which accepted leadership images present women is to move increasing numbers of women into leadership positions in the hope that, over time, as women leaders become less rare there will be a shift in our norms of leadership. But without a more thorough-going attention to the masculinity of organizational dynamics, and faced with research results that suggest little real difference between men's and women's leadership styles *in conventional organizations*, feminists question whether simply adding women in key positions will be enough to bring about so fundamental a change. Feminists would also want to raise the question of whether feminine leadership styles simply mask hierarchy more effectively; they would want to explore whether we need leaders at all—in the sense of someone who defines the meaning of situations, shows others the right way to approach problems, and makes them want what the leader wants (i.e., motivates them). From this perspective, it may be that the perceived need for leadership is a function of hierarchy, which socializes those in the lower ranks to believe that they are incapable of contributing to a joint effort to decide what to do, or that if they do have viewpoints, they had better follow the chain of command. Kelley's (1989) ideas, although not ostensibly feminist, are consistent with what many feminists would advocate. He suggests that people in work settings form small leaderless groups in which each member of the group assumes equal responsibility for achieving goals, or alternatively, that groups rotate the leadership role. Kelley notes, "Some of these temporary leaders will be less effective than others, of course, and some may be weak indeed . . . [but] experience of the leadership role is essential to the education of effective followers" (p. 133).

Existing organizational norms of efficiency will make forming and sustaining leaderless groups difficult. Conventional wisdom sees hierarchy as the inevitable form for complex organizations in postindustrial society, a view that blocks consideration of alternative forms and practices as impractical or unrealistic. Even discussions of the new entrepreneurial, flexible, participative form of management assume that there will have to be a leader to keep the mission on track, and most of the delegation and decentralization that goes on is carefully restricted. In addition, most organizational members continue to be somewhat uncomfortable with the structureless feeling a leaderless group evokes. In teaching, I have observed that when I ask my classes to decide how to organize their activities for a particular class, even 10 minutes (out of a 3-hour class) spent working out a process that everyone can live with begins to seem like a waste of time to many members of the class, and I find myself growing internally nervous about being seen as indecisive. Thus I am aware of how far we are in complex organizations from being able to practice ideas like leaderless groups or rotating leadership. I do believe, however, that if we were to cease assuming, even for a little while or in a limited arena, that organizations or societal systems "need" leadership, we might make room for some fresh perspectives to emerge. In public administration, putting a hold on such assumptions might give us the opportunity to question the power implications in ideas about the need for administrators to lead a system of government that, from the bureaucrat's perspective, may appear fractionated and inefficient but that, from the perspective of ordinary citizens, is much more likely to seem like a monolithic juggernaut. Could we make room, for example, for an image of administrative leadership that includes facilitating a share in organizational decision making for agency clients, for citizens, and for secretaries and clerks?

Virtue

The feminist perspective on virtue takes a somewhat different tack from the revisions of competence and leadership. In the first two cases, the problem was one of cultural masculinity masquerading as universality, blocking nonconforming people and their ideas. In discussions of virtue in public administration, we do find masculine images—the guardian, the seeker of fame, the hero—but in the idea of virtue itself we can perceive a latent femininity that these images unconsciously attempt to mask. The refashioning of American ideas about virtue during the founding period transformed it from a culturally masculine quality expressed in the public actions of civic-minded citizens to a trait inculcated by women in the home and practiced in private acts of benevolence. This transformation of virtue feminized it, particularly in contrast to the masculine assertive pursuit of rational self-interest in the world of business. In order for public administration to resuscitate the notion of *public* virtue, then, masculine images have been brought to bear. The guardian or protector of the people is a father figure, turning the unruly masses into a loyal and obedient flock. The Hamilton seeker of fame and honor is a paternal, ambitious, and Olympian actor before a public audience, dependent on women to handle necessities like food and child rearing but repressing their significance in favor of a quest for immortality. The hero is typically a commanding figure with a masculinity that extends back to the time of the ancient Greeks.

From a feminist perspective, the idea of virtue will remain problematic as long as the dependence of the public sphere on the domestic sphere—and the sexual division of labor that goes with it—continues unacknowledged. Publicness, including public virtue, has excluded and silenced women for centuries. The public space has been a male preserve, an arrangement that made it possible for the American founders to enthrone self-interest and expel virtue by associating the one with men and the other with women. *Public virtue* thus involves a reuniting of masculinity and femininity. Unless we are able to approach the project of promoting the virtue of public administrators in light of that assumption, we will continue to struggle with the apparent "weakness" of virtue: It will continue to seem soft, sentimental, or (most damning of all) unrealistic.

Of all the current images of the virtuous public administrator, the idea of the administrator-as-citizen comes closest to an understanding consistent with a feminist perspective; however, this feminist, at least, would want to move Cooper's idea of the administrator as "citizen for the rest of us" to "citizen *with* the rest of us." Why could we not come to see the place of the public administrator in American governance as special not for its elevation but for its centrality? Based on such a vision, public administrators deserve our approbation not because they understand the public interest better than the rest of us but because they are willing to bear more of the burden of facilitating its accomplishment. As facilitators, their role is to make the governance process as inclusive as possible, particularly of those whose interests and needs are poorly represented in interest group politics (Gray & Chapin, 1998; Stivers, 1990a). To fulfill this role, the administrator-as-citizen sees herself or himself as "partner with" rather than "guardian over" or "citizen for"—one who occupies a location in the web of government that gives her or him not only access to sharable information but also a boundary-spanning capacity, both of which can be used to empower others (Stivers, 1990b).

Like the midwife in the case of expertise, a domestic image that might reunite public and private images of virtue is Ruddick's (1989) idea of motherhood as "fostering growth," or "nurturing a child's developing spirit." Ruddick argues that children require this nurturing because of the complexity of their developmental process; she points out that the central maternal tasks entailed in fostering growth are *administrative*, requiring the organization of effort in the face of the many destabilizing influences in children's lives. Ruddick argues that, while the fostering of growth entails a great deal of routine, sometimes exhausting, work, it is at the same time fascinating and rewarding. Ruddick suggests that fostering growth requires a "metaphysical attitude" that both holds close and welcomes change, one that sees children as "constructive agents of their world and their life in it" (pp. 82–93). Thus we have a maternal image that matches in many ways the lives and responsibilities of virtuous public administrators: Like mothers, they must foster growth under conditions of complexity; like mothers, they must perform both routine and rewarding work in the interest of others who are in a sense their responsibility; like mothers, they must both hold close (conserve administrative resources and capacities) and welcome change; just as mothers see their children as agents of their own lives, so must public administrators see citizens in the same light.

The general emphasis in the feminist perspective is on horizontal rather than vertical relations: on seeing oneself as reaching across rather than down, on seeing others as respected equals rather than threats to one's own autonomy or sheep in need of herding. This perspective also entails viewing the conceptual division between public and domestic spheres as permeable and mutually supportive. The intention here is not to promote governmental control over the intimate aspects of our lives— for indeed, a seemingly hard and fast line between private and public has never prevented governments from controlling the bodies of women, it has only rationalized the exclusion of women from public life. Instead, the intent is to make explicit the reliance of governance—of individual and group action in public—on the support that governing (in fact all) individuals receive (or are presumed to receive) at home: the shelter, food, clothing, rearing, nurturing, and comfort that make life livable. Awareness of the mutuality of public and domestic spheres should lead us to demand equal sharing of the work in the two sectors by men and women, thus to understandings of them (sectors and sexes) as equally important. As long as public administrators assert their rightful share in ruling a special public sphere that depends on but denigrates the domestic, they will be laying claim to a sphere that puts women in their place and thus perpetuating a weak understanding of virtue.

History

We saw that women played an integral part in 19th-century benevolent work and in governmental reform efforts, both of which were significant forces in the development of the administrative state. When turn-of-the century governments began to take on new responsibilities, much of what they began to do was women's work (redefined as "social service"), and it was at women's behest that they began to do it. Women were able to offer a viable alternative to the rationalizing vision of "the city as a business" put forward by male reformers; they saw the city as a home for its people. Although giving women's involvement in reform its due is certainly important, its significance extends to the conceptual shift that such awareness makes necessary. We see that historically the central tension in public administration between values (benevolence, democracy, the public) and techniques (efficiency, administration) is pervaded with gender implications: Just as the developing field of public administration was unable to accommodate the views of women, so today the field continues to sacrifice democracy on the altar of efficiency. In the accepted way of things, the ultimate practical question is this: How much participation (or process, or feeling) can we afford?

Thus a feminist approach to public administration entails a reexamination of its history, not only to give women their rightful place as full participants in setting the administrative state on its course but to understand the gender dimensions implicit in its most central ideas and the interests that are thereby served. As Scott (1989) observes, history, which is preeminently the history of politics and government, has been "enacted on the field of gender" (p. 100). Gender is both "a constitutive element of social relationships" (p. 94) and "a primary field . . . by means of which power is articulated" (p. 95). If so, it is clear that public administration, as both a configuration of social relationships and an institution of public power, needs gender as a category of analysis in order to be more completely delineated. Just as we now accept the impossibility of understanding the practice of public administration stripped of its political and economic context, so we must recognize that attention to the influence of gender, race, and class are fundamental to comprehension not only of present-day concepts but of their lineage, their historical development. Clearly, gendered ideas (not always recognized as such) have contributed to defenses of the administrative state since its inception. A feminist approach to the history of public administration and its theory is thus not a matter of interest only to women (and thus relegated to the realm of women's studies) but central to a full understanding of the field.

Case in point: the gender dimensions in the tension between efficiency and democracy, revealed in the Progressive era spectacle of womanly benevolence invaded by masculine (businesslike) methods and in men's efforts to purge reform arguments, such as those in favor of administration, of any taint of sentimentality. Although theorists of public administration tend to treat the democracy-efficiency issue as a matter of rational argument, the lens of gender would suggest that the rationality of the discussion is "bounded," to use Herbert Simon's well-known term, but in a manner that never occurred to Simon. It may be that the tendency in public administration to treat democracy as a cost of doing business, tolerable only to the extent that efficiency allows, reflects nonconscious homage to masculinity. In the absence of this awareness, proponents of democratic administrative practice will continue to have trouble explaining why persuasion that appeals solely to cognitive capacities continues to have so little effect.

Another implication of women's part in the history of public administration has to do with coming to terms with diversity. History suggests that integrating gender—as well as race and class—into thinking in public administration will entail more than simply bringing differences into the fold, that is, turning them to the service of established administrative interests. During the 19th century, women's philanthropic activities came under increasing pressure to become efficient and were finally absorbed by an administrative state that viewed efficiency with reverence. Ever since, womanly benevolence has been frequently on tap but never on top; thus one side of a dichotomy took control of the other, requiring it to subsume its nature in order to survive. A gender analysis of public administration's history, then, suggests that dealing effectively with what appear to be either-or choices will involve what Follett (1918) calls an "interweaving of willings" (p. 69). Follett viewed diversity not only as inevitable but as a positive force in life. She argued that it was a great mistake to try to get rid of diversity: "Fear of difference is dread of life itself. . . . One of the greatest values of controversy is its revealing nature. The real issues come out in the open and have the possibility of being reconciled" (Follett, 1924, p. 204). Follett would tell us now, I believe, that public administration needs to risk a truly open dialogue, one in which differences are encouraged rather than papered over, one that therefore constitutes "co-creating . . . [that is,] the core of democracy, the essence of citizenship" (p. 302).

The Administrative State

Women's perspective on the administrative state is much more likely to be developed sitting in the secretarial pool or on one side or the other of the caseworker's desk than it is as a member of the Senior Executive Service. A feminist approach to public administration means examining the material realities of women's place in the bureaucracy and the barriers they face to fuller participation, which as we have seen include both glass ceilings and glass walls. Thinking about personnel policies cannot confine itself to issues such as how to respond to "employee demands" for day care (as if the adequate care of children had no public interest dimension) or to facile comments about how much the agency relies on its support staff (without paying them in line with the level of its dependence). We must move to an investigation of how a refusal to take such material realities into account has limited our thinking. Because much of the management literature in public administration journals and textbooks shows no apparent consciousness that there are two sexes in organizations or that their respective experiences are in any way different, the opportunities for new approaches are limitless. We might start by changing the tone of the discussions about the "diverse workforce," from considering it a looming problem to thinking of it as a promising new capacity. Next, we might spend time reflecting on (instead of denying) the existence of sexual dynamics in the bureaucracy as well as the extent to which conscious or unconscious racism and sexism hinder the progress of diverse employees and block changes in the terms of organizational life. No public manager should practice without becoming educated about these issues and without developing awareness of his or her personal implication in them. No theorist should develop a model of managerial excellence that does not include sensitivity to and skill in dealing with gender issues, including the disparity between norms of expertise and leadership and expectations about proper sex-role behavior and the dilemma that this disparity poses for women managers.

In addition, a feminist perspective on the administrative state would encourage theory to come to terms with depersonalized power. The claim to administrative discretion is the claim to power on the basis of technical, managerial, and moral expertise. The discretionary judgments of administrators are said to be justifiable because they make decisions on the basis of more objective knowledge, clearer vision, higher principles, or a deeper commitment to wrestling with the tough questions of public life than do other citizens. This claim to power is asserted on the basis that the arena in which it is exercised is distinctive because it is public. But as we have seen, a discrete public sector maintains its boundaries (therefore its exceptionalism) at the expense of women. A feminist interpretation of administrative discretion and of the power inherent in it must therefore begin by calling into question the accepted model of discretionary judgment—that is, as McSwite (1997) has shown, by questioning the very idea that we citizens have to leave governing up to Men of Reason.

Feminist Practical Wisdom

The idea of discretionary judgment provides a good opportunity to explore in more depth the theoretical implications of feminism in public administration because it draws together themes of competence, leadership, and virtue that have permeated this examination of public administration theory and links them to the exercise of power.

One theory of discretion presents it in terms of the exercise of practical wisdom (*phronesis*), an Aristotelian idea that brings to bear intellectual and moral capacities on public questions. Morgan (1990) argues that public administrators possess phronesis, "a special kind of prudence . . . that enables them to coalesce considerations of workability, [popular] acceptability, and fit" with constitutional principles and other key community values. In the American system of government, "it is the deliberative capacity to know how to make the right thing work" (p. 74). Morgan says that this capacity includes the ability to take the broader and longer view and a public-interested and constitutionally based understanding of the agency's perspective. Morgan and Kass's (1991) research suggests that in actual decision making, the practical wisdom of administrators takes the form of subordinating standards of technical competence and the resolution of competing claims to constitutional principles as administrators interpret them.

To develop a feminist perspective on this notion of practical wisdom, we have to start by examining the Aristotelian origins of the idea, because Aristotle himself believed women incapable of exercising the form of public judgment that theorists like Morgan now advocate as a model. As we have seem, feminism is interested in questioning the roots of ideas to determine whether in the present day they still contain dimensions that work against the interests of women. When we look at what Aristotle had to say about practical wisdom and also what he had to say about women, we see that a considerable tension exists, one that has ramifications in our own time.

Aristotle's (1976) idea of *phronesis* entails the ability "to deliberate rightly about . . . what is conducive to the good life generally" (Sec. 1140a24); therefore, it blends intellectual and moral capacities. Practical wisdom is acquired through experience at assessing situations in order to determine which elements are relevant to making the right decision; thus it has perceptual as well as rational dimensions. It also involves the emotions; without them, we might miss relevant aspects of situations. *Phronesis* is preeminently a public quality, practiced by those who rule, including citizens.

Aristotle held that women's natural capacities included sexual reproduction and household duties and precluded citizenship. Not only are women suited only for household and child-rearing duties, however, but their realm, though crucial to survival, is inferior to the public world of male citizens (Okin, 1979; Saxonhouse, 1985; Sherman, 1989). Thus, admitting women to the company of the practically wise requires a fundamental adjustment in Aristotelian notions of the good society and the good life, which are predicated on a sharp separation between public and private.

The root of the problem is that Aristotle's idea of practical wisdom makes it a capacity developed and exercised in public. The essence of citizenship is to interact with fellow citizens in the public space: to listen and speak, to see and be seen, above all to act virtuously (that is, in support of the common good). In Aristotle's scheme, women are barred from this life. But more serious than that, the viability of men's public life depends on the exclusion of women and slaves: In the balanced and stable society, someone must take the responsibility for managing the necessities of existence if the ultimate good—the leisured political life not bound by the need for results—is to be realized.

But the difficulty goes even deeper, for we are not faced with a vision of society made up of separate but equal spheres, men ruling in public life, women in private. In Aristotle's society, men dominated in both spheres. The household is a hierarchy in order that the polis need not be. Furthermore, the domination that exists within the household is, by definition, not political; therefore, questions about the justice of household arrangements cannot arise. Such practical wisdom as a wife attains is a stunted variety, limited to the lesser concerns of survival.

If practical wisdom requires political practice for its fullest expression and if political practice is only viable given its separation from a realm devoted exclusively to sustenance, then practical wisdom itself depends on this bifurcation between polis and household and the subordination of the one to the other. In Aristotle's scheme of things, the household's most notable function is to free men from the exigencies of existence so that they can practice citizenship. The freedom of some, therefore, is purchased at the cost of the unfreedom of others—women and slaves.

In assessing the usefulness of the concept of *phronesis* today, then, when public and private are still (although somewhat less absolutely) divided and when women still bear the primary burden of household affairs, feminists would want to insist that the idea will remain problematic until women are as free as men (in practical terms as well as in theory) to participate in public deliberations and until men bear an equal responsibility with women for the necessities of life.

The characteristics of *phronesis* are nevertheless interesting from a feminist perspective. Many of the qualities of practical wisdom are strikingly consistent with historically and culturally woman-centered ideas; for example, the rejection of narrow abstracted rationalism in favor of a broader form that encompasses the emotions (a dimension that current theorists neglect), the stress on the contextuality of practical knowledge and its basis in concrete experience, the acknowledged impossibility of depending solely on rules acquired through formal training and hence the inconsistency with ideas of professional control over events and processes, and the interactive nature of its exercise.

Feminists would want to preserve and promote these qualities in public administrative practice. But they would go further and urge a rendering that severs *phronesis* from dependence on the public-domestic split. Feminists would want an understanding of practical wisdom that acknowledges the embodied character of public sector deliberation and action. As Patterson (2001) observes, "the center part of the word 'embodiment' urges us to think of bodies as literal, particular, mortal entities of meat and action," in contrast to the tendency in public administration to "take people out of time, place, and social relation, and figure their bodies mainly, or only, as image" (p. 177). We need to recognize that most if not all of the concerns of public administration deal with the sustenance and survival of the polity and its individual members. If so, a posture of emotional distance is less appropriate than one that entails engaged objectivity, embodied reason, and the integration of feeling and thought. Harrison (1985) argues that dualistic thinking in moral discourse presents us with apparently irreconcilable alternatives; instead, she says, in a suggestion reminiscent of Follett, the essence of justice is a condition under which both my fulfillment and yours become possible. Harrison suggests that at the roots of zero-sum thinking lie patterns of privilege and domination. From her perspective, cutting oneself off from the material conditions of life make one less rather than more qualified for ethical deliberation. Her views expose an inconsistency in Aristotle's idea of *phronesis*, for it would seem that so context-dependent a form of wisdom requires connection rather than distancing from everyday life, including the household, in order to acquire the experience that builds wisdom.

The context in which feminist practical wisdom is grounded includes the influence of gender, race, and class on the life chances of members of the polity; feminist *phronesis* seeks connection with marginalized people in order to ground practice in the real conditions of their lives. Harrison (1985) urges us to resist the temptation to universalize social relations; rather, she says, "moral clarification requires careful attention . . . to the particularity and contingency of human action and social-cultural experience" (p. 65). She reminds us that what is practical in particular about feminist practical wisdom is its roots in and commitment to integrating (as Follett would put it) the experiences and perspectives of diverse people.

A feminist perspective on practical wisdom also requires us to examine its institutional framework. Just as Aristotle envisioned the fullest expression of *phronesis* to entail not simply addressing an individual's personal dilemmas but working out the meaning of the common good in the context of citizenship, so feminist practical wisdom calls on the public administrator to become critically reflective about the agency context within which she or he practices. As a result of women's historical exclusion from the public sector, a theme in feminism has been the significance of silences and secrets—of that which is denied, suppressed, excluded. In examining the details of particular issues facing an agency, one must look beyond the overt to that which is usually ignored, not talked about, taken for granted. One must question business as usual, the accounts people typically give of their actions. In doing so, however, the practically wise public administrator is likely to encounter dissonance between marginalized needs and perspectives and existing institutional policies and patterns of behavior—a dilemma that may frequently beset with personal risk the decision about what it is right to do given the circumstances.

Yet in administrative decision making guided by feminist practical wisdom, the others one serves, the others one works with, become not abstracted but concrete persons with whom one is in relationship. Therefore, they become not just sources of knowledge to guide individual decision making but collaborators in a joint project of discovery and definition or redefinition. Thus, the feminist charge to public administration is to take seriously an idea of administrative discretion that is concrete, situational, experience based, interactive, and collaborative and grounded in perception and feeling as well as in rational analysis. What feminists ask of discretionary judgment in the public sector is to reject public-private, self-other dichotomies. Such conceptual dualisms restrict women's access to the public space and block the transformative power of historically woman-centered ideas. Until we are free of such imprisoning ways of thinking, public administration will continue to be implicated in gender dynamics that work hardships in women's lives and to estrange itself from the very intellectual and spiritual sources it needs to nourish a truly practical wisdom.

Conclusion

This chapter has tried to suggest some of the starting or entry points through which an analysis of public administration through the lens of gender might begin to reshape the practice and the field as we know them. All the answers are far from obvious at this point; besides, for one person to attempt a full-blown vision of public administration transformed by feminist thinking would be somewhat overweening and, perhaps more important, a contradiction in terms. This feminist, at least, is skeptical of overarching visions for their tendency to put people in their proper places and/or cancel out their own ideas and dreams. I have introduced some different notions into the ongoing conversation in public administration in the hope that they will stimulate people to examine for themselves the gender dilemmas that lie in terms, concepts, and ideas in good currency. A decade after the first edition, there has been less attention to gender in theory and practice than I once hoped, but the transformational potential of such conversations remains for us to find.

Granted, if we put feminist ideas to work in the field, quite fundamental changes could occur. One cannot raise questions like the necessity of hierarchy or the unjust implications of the separation between public and private without opening up world-shifting vistas. But I would not make the decision about how far we should pursue these possibilities even if I could. Transformation will happen not as the result of selecting the future on a grand scale but will evolve out of countless conversations and situations that bring people together around particular problems. On the other hand, it is possible that the reluctance of people in public administration to take up questions of gender can be traced to a sense, often only partly conscious, of just how fundamental these questions are.

Ultimately, then, this book still serves as an invitation to others who care about public administration. Let us not deny the existence of gender dimensions in our images and ideas and the dilemmas they pose for women—and for men as well. Let us deal with them.

References

Abelson, R. (1999, July 14). Women and minorities not getting to the top. *New York Times*, p. C4.

Ackelsberg, M. A., & Shanley, M. L. (1996). Privacy, publicity, and power: A feminist rethinking of the public-private distinction. In N. J. Hirschmann & C. Di Stefano (Eds.), *Revisioning the political: Feminist reconstructions of traditional concepts in Western political theory* (pp. 213–233). Boulder, CO: Westview.

Adair, D. (1974). *Fame and the founding fathers* (T. Colbourn, Ed.). New York: Norton.

Addams, J. (1935). *My friend Julia Lathrop*. New York: Macmillan.

Allen, D. G. (1987). Professionalism, occupational segregation by gender, and control of nursing. *Women and Politics, 7*, 1–24.

Allen, R. L. (1983). *Reluctant reformers: Racism and social reform movements in the United States*. Washington, DC: Howard University Press.

Allen, W. H. (1907). *Efficient democracy*. New York: Dodd, Mead.

Allen, W. H. (1913). *Women's part in government whether she votes or not*. New York: Dodd, Mead.

Alvesson, M., & Billing, Y. D. (1997). *Understanding gender and organizations*. Thousand Oaks, CA: Sage.

Andolsen, B. H. (1986). *"Daughters of Jefferson, daughters of bootblacks": Racism and American feminism*. Macon, GA: Mercer University Press.

Arendt, H. (1958). *The human condition*. Chicago and London: University of Chicago Press.

Argyris, C. (1957). *Personality and organization*. New York: Harper.

Aristotle. (1976). *The Nichomachean ethics* (J. A. K. Thompson, Trans.). Harmondsworth, UK: Penguin.

Aristotle. (1981). *The politics* (T. A. Sinclair, Trans.). Harmondsworth, UK: Penguin.

Aron, C. S. (1987). *Ladies and gentlemen of the civil service: Middle class workers in Victorian America*. New York: Oxford University Press.

Astin, H. S., & Leland, C. (1991). *Women of influence, women of vision: A cross-generational study of leaders and social change*. San Francisco: Jossey-Bass.

Baker, P. (1990). The domestication of politics: Women and American political society, 1780–1920. In L. Gordon (Ed.), *Women, the state, and welfare* (pp. 55–91). Madison: University of Wisconsin Press.

Baker, R. S. (1968). *Woodrow Wilson: Life and letters. Vol. 4: President, 1913–1914.* New York: Greenwood. (Original work published 1931)

Barnard, C. I. (1938). *The functions of the executive.* Cambridge, MA: Harvard University Press.

Barnard, C. I. (1948). *Organization and management: Selected papers.* Cambridge, MA: Harvard University Press.

Barrileaux, C., Feiock, R., & Crew, R. (1992). Indicators and correlates of American states' administrative characteristics. *State and Local Government Review, 24*(1), 12–18.

Barringer, F. (2001, July 15). The lost privacy of Gary Condit. *New York Times,* Sec. 4, p. 3.

Beard, C. A. (1916, March). Training for efficient public service. *Annals of the American Academy of Political and Social Science, 64,* 215–226.

Beard, M. R. (1915, April). Woman's work for the city. *National Municipal Review, 4,* 204–210.

Behn, R. D. (1998). What right do public managers have to lead? *Public Administration Review, 58*(3), 209–230.

Bellavita, C. (1986, Fall). The organization of leadership. *The Bureaucrat,* pp. 13–16.

Bellavita, C. (1991). The public administrator as hero. *Administration & Society, 23*(2), 155–185.

Bem, S. L. (1994, August 17). In a male-centered world, female differences are transformed into female disadvantages. *The Chronicle of Higher Education,* pp. B1–B3.

Bennett, J. (2001, January 14). CEO-USA. *New York Times Magazine,* pp. 24–28, 49, 54, 57, 59–60.

Bennis, W. G., & Nanus, B. (1985). *Leaders: The strategy for taking charge.* New York: Harper & Row.

Biernat, M., & Wortman, C. B. (1991). Sharing of home responsibilities between professionally employed women and their husbands. *Journal of Personality and Social Psychology, 60*(6), 844–860.

Blagdon, H. W. (1967). *Woodrow Wilson: The academic years.* Cambridge, MA: Belknap Press.

Blair, S. L., & Lichter, D. T. (1991). Measuring the division of household labor: Gender segregation of housework among American couples. *Journal of Family Issues, 12*(1), 91–113.

Bledstein, B. J. (1976). *The culture of professionalism: The middle class and the development of higher education in America.* New York: Norton.

Bloch, R. H. (1987). The gendered meanings of virtue in revolutionary America. *Signs: Journal of Women in Culture and Society, 13*(1), 37–58.

Blum, L. A. (1988). Moral exemplars: Reflections on Schindler, the Trocmes, and others. *Midwest Studies in Philosophy, 12,* 196–221.

Bologh, R. W. (1990). *Love or greatness: Max Weber and masculine thinking— a feminist inquiry.* London: Unwin Hyman.

Bordo, S. (1987). The Cartesian masculinization of thought. In S. Harding & J. F. O'Barr (Eds.), *Sex and scientific inquiry* (pp. 247–264). Chicago: University of Chicago Press.

Bowling, C. J., & Wright, D. S. (1998). Change and continuity in state administration: Administrative leadership across four decades. *Public Administration Review, 58*(5), 429–444.

Bowlker, (Mrs.) T. J. (1912, June). Woman's home-making function applied to the municipality. *American City, 6,* 863–869.

Braudy, L. (1986). *The frenzy of renown: Fame and its history.* New York: Oxford University Press.

Breckinridge, S. P. (Ed.). (1927). *Public welfare administration in the United States: Selected documents.* Chicago: University of Chicago Press.

Brooks-Higginbotham, E. (1989). The problem of race in women's history. In E. Weed (Ed.), *Coming to terms: Feminism, theory, politics* (pp. 122–133). New York: Routledge.

Brooks-Higginbotham, E. (1993). *Righteous discontent: The women's movement in the black Baptist church, 1880–1920.* Cambridge, MA: Harvard University Press.

Brown, W. (1988). *Manhood and politics: A feminist reading in political theory.* Totowa, NJ: Rowman & Littlefield.

Bruere, H. (1912). *The new city government: A discussion of municipal administration based on a survey of ten commission-governed cities.* New York and London: D. Appleton.

Butler, M. (1978). Early liberal roots of feminism: John Locke and the attack on patriarchy. *American Political Science Review, 72,* 135–150.

Caldwell, L. K. (1988). *The administrative theories of Hamilton and Jefferson: Their contribution to thought on public administration* (2nd ed.). New York: Holmes & Meier.

Carby, H. V. (1986). On the threshold of the women's era: Lynching, empire, and sexuality in black feminist theory. In H. L. Gates, Jr. (Ed.), *Race, writing and difference* (pp. 301–316). Chicago: University of Chicago Press.

Carli, L. L., & Eagly, A. H. (1999). Gender effects on social influence and emergent leadership. In G. N. Powell (Ed.), *Handbook of gender and work* (pp. 203–222). Thousand Oaks, CA: Sage.

Chodorow, N. (1978). *The reproduction of mothering: Psychoanalysis and the sociology of gender.* Berkeley: University of California Press.

Cigler, B. A. (1990). Public administration and the paradox of professionalism. *Public Administration Review, 50*(6), 637–653.

Clark, L. M. G. (1979). Women and Locke: Who owns the apple in the garden of Eden? In L. M. G. Clark & L. Lange (Eds.), *The sexism of social and political theory: Women and reproduction from Plato to Nietzsche* (pp. 16–40). Toronto: University of Toronto Press.

Clarke, L. M. G., & Lange, L. (Eds.). (1979). *The sexism of social and political theory: Women and reproduction from Plato to Nietzsche.* Toronto: University of Toronto Press.

Cleveland, F. A. (1909). *Chapters on municipal administration and accounting.* New York: Longmans, Green.

Cleveland, F. A. (1913). *Organized democracy.* New York: Longmans, Green.

Clinton, C. (1984). *The other civil war: American women in the nineteenth century.* New York: Hill & Wang.

Cocks, J. (1989). *The oppositional imagination: Feminism, critique, and political theory.* London: Routledge.

Connolly, W. E. (1993). *The terms of political discourse* (3rd ed.). Princeton, NJ: Princeton University Press.

Cook, B. J. (1998). Politics, political leadership, and public management. *Public Administration Review, 58*(3), 225–230.

Cooke, J. E. (Ed.). (1961). *The federalist.* Middletown, CT: Wesleyan University Press.

Cooper, T. L. (1984a). Citizenship and professionalism in public administration [Special issue] (H. G. Frederickson & R. C. Chandler, Eds.), *Public Administration Review, 44,* 143–149.

Cooper, T. L. (1984b). Public administration in an age of scarcity: A citizenship role for public administrators. In J. Rabin & J. S. Bowman (Eds.), *Politics and administration: Woodrow Wilson and American public administration* (pp. 297–314). New York: Marcel Dekker.

Cooper, T. L. (1991). *A ethic of citizenship for public administration.* Englewood Cliffs, NJ: Prentice Hall.

Cooper, T. L. (1992). On virtue. In T. L. Cooper & N. D. Wright (Eds.), *Exemplary public administrators: Character and leadership in government* (pp. 1–8). San Francisco: Jossey-Bass.

Cooper, T. L., & Wright, N. D. (Eds.). (1992). *Exemplary public administrators: Character and leadership in government.* San Francisco: Jossey-Bass.

Cott, N. F. (1977). *The bonds of womanhood: Women's sphere in New England, 1780–1830.* New Haven, CT: Yale University Press.

Crenson, M. A. (1975). *The federal machine: Beginnings of bureaucracy in Jacksonian America.* Baltimore: Johns Hopkins University Press.

Croly, H. (1963). *The promise of American life.* New York: E. P. Dutton. (Original work published 1909).

Davis, A. J. (1984). *Spearheads for reform: The social settlement and the Progressive movement, 1880–1914* (2nd ed.). New Brunswick, NJ: Rutgers University Press.

Deardorff, N. R. (1914, November). Women in municipal activities. *Annals of the American Academy of Political and Social Science, 56,* 71–77.

De Beauvoir, S. (1961). *The second sex* (H. M. Parshley, Trans.). New York: Bantam.

DeHoog, R., & Whitaker, G. (1993). Professional leadership in local government. *International Journal of Public Administration, 16*(12), 2033–2049.

Derber, C. (1983). Managing professionals: Ideological proletarianization and post-industrial labor. *Theory and Society, 12,* 309–341.

DeWitt, K. (1995, November 23). Job bias cited for minorities and women. *New York Times,* p. B14.

Dobel, J. P. (1998). Judging the private lives of public officials. *Administration & Society, 30,* 115–142.

Dobrzynski, J. H. (1996, February 28). Gaps and barriers, and women's careers. *New York Times,* p. C2.

Doig, J. W. (1988). *Leadership and innovation in the administrative state.* Paper presented at the Minnowbrook II meeting, Minnowbrook, NY.

Doig, J. W., & Hargrove, E. C. (Eds.). (1987). *Leadership and innovation: A biographical perspective on entrepreneurs in government.* Baltimore: Johns Hopkins University Press.

Dolan, J. (2000). The Senior Executive Service: Gender, attitudes, and representative bureaucracy. *Journal of Public Administration Research and Theory, 10*(3), 513–530.

Dudley, L. (1996). Fencing in the inherently governmental debate. In G. Wamsley & J. Wolf (Eds.), *Refounding democratic public administration: Modern paradoxes, postmodern challenges* (pp. 68–91). Thousand Oaks, CA: Sage.

Edwards, L. R. (1984). *Psyche as hero: Female heroism and fictional form.* Middletown, CT: Wesleyan University Press.

Edwards, R. (1997). *Angels in the machinery: Gender in American party politics from the Civil War to the Progressive era.* New York: Oxford University Press.

Epstein, C. F. (1988). *Deceptive distinctions: Sex, gender and the social order.* New Haven, CT: Yale University Press.

Etzioni, A. (1969). *The semi-professions and their organizations.* New York: Free Press.

Ferguson, K. (1984). *The feminist case against bureaucracy.* Philadelphia: Temple University Press.

Few women found in top public jobs. (1992, January 3). *New York Times,* p. A8.

Fierman, J. (1990, July). Why women still don't hit the top. *Fortune,* pp. 30, 40–42, 50, 54, 58, 62.

Finer, H. (1940). Administrative responsibility in democratic government. In C. Friedrich (Ed.), *Public policy* (pp. 247–275). Cambridge, MA: Harvard University Press.

Finley, M. I. (1965). *The world of Odysseus* (Rev. ed.). New York: Viking.

Fisher, B. (1988). Wandering in the wilderness: The search for women role models. *Signs: Journal of Women in Culture and Society, 13*(2), 211–233.

Fitzpatrick, E. (1990). *Endless crusade: Women social scientists and Progressive reform.* New York: Oxford University Press.

Fletcher, J. (1999). *Disappearing acts: Gender, power and relational practice.* Cambridge: MIT Press.

Follett, M. P. (1918). *The new state.* London: Longmans, Green.

Follett, M. P. (1924). *Creative experience.* New York and London: Longmans, Green.

Fondas, N. (1997). Feminization unveiled: Management qualities in contemporary writings. *Academy of Management Review, 22*(1), 257–282.

Fox, C., & Cochran, C. E. (1990). Discretionary public administration: Toward a Platonic guardian class. In H. Kass & B. Catron (Eds.), *Images and identities in public administration* (pp. 87–112). Newbury Park, CA: Sage.

Franzway, S., Court, D., & Connell, R. W. (1989). *Staking a claim: Feminism, bureaucracy, and the state.* Sydney: Allen & Unwin.

Fraser, N. (1990). Talking about needs: Interpretive contests as political conflicts. In C. R. Sunstein (Ed.), *Feminism and political theory* (pp. 159–181). Chicago: University of Chicago Press.

Frederickson, H. G., & Hart, D. K. (1985). The public service and the patriotism of benevolence. *Public Administration Review, 45*(5), 547–554.

Friedrich, C. J. (1940). Public power and the nature of administrative responsibility. In C. Friedrich (Ed.), *Public policy* (pp. 221–245). Cambridge, MA: Harvard University Press.

Frye, M. (1996). The possibility of feminist theory. In A. Garry & M. Pearsall (Eds.), *Women, knowledge, and reality: Explorations in feminist philosophy* (pp. 34–47). New York and London: Routledge.

Gawthrop, L. A. (1984). Civis, civitas, and civilitas: A new focus for the year 2000. [Special issue] (H. G. Frederickson & R. C. Chandler (Eds.), *Public Administration Review, 44*, 101–107.

Giddings, P. (1985). *When and where I enter: The impact of black women on race and sex in America.* New York: Bantam.

Gilligan, C. (1982). *In a different voice: Psychological theory and women's development.* Cambridge, MA: Harvard University Press.

Ginzberg, L. D. (1990). *Women and the work of benevolence: Morality, politics, and class in the 19th century United States.* New Haven, CT: Yale University Press.

Glazer, P. M., & Slater, M. (1987). *Unequal colleagues: The entrance of women into the professions, 1890–1940.* New Brunswick, NJ: Rutgers University Press.

Goodnow, F. J. (1900). *Politics and administration.* New York: Macmillan.

Gordon, L. (Ed.). (1990). *Women, the state, and welfare.* Madison: University of Wisconsin Press.

Gray, J., & Chapin, L. (1998). Targeted community initiative: "Putting citizens first!" In C. King, C. Stivers, & Collaborators, *Government is us: Public administration in an anti-government era* (pp. 175–194). Thousand Oaks, CA: Sage.

Green, R., Keller, L., & Wamsley, G. (1993). Reconstituting a profession for American public administration. *Public Administration Review, 53*(6), 516–524.

Green, R. T. (1988). The Hamiltonian image of the public administrator: Public administrators as prudent constitutionalists. *Dialogue: The Public Administration Theory Network, 10*(3), 25–53.

Grenier, G. (1988*). Inhuman relations: Quality circles and anti-unionism in American industry.* Philadelphia: Temple University Press.

Grosz, E. (1990). *Jacques Lacan: A feminist introduction.* London: Routledge.

Grubb, B. (1991, Winter). The quiet revolution of Bev Forbes. *Seattle University News,* pp. 18–19.

Gulick, L. (1937). Notes on the theory of organization. In L. Gulick & L. Urwick (Eds.), *Papers on the science of administration.* New York: Institute of Public Administration.

Gutek, B. (1989). Sexuality in the workplace: Key issues in social research and organizational practice. In J. Hearn, D. L. Sheppard, P. Tancred-Sheriff, & G. Burrell (Eds.), *The sexuality of organization* (pp. 56–70). London: Sage.

Haber, S. (1964). *Efficiency and uplift: Scientific management in the Progressive era, 1890–1920.* Chicago: University of Chicago Press.

Hale, M. M., & Kelly, R. M. (Eds.). (1989). *Gender, bureaucracy, and democracy: Careers and equal opportunity in the public sector.* Westport, CT: Greenwood.

Harding, S. (1986). *The science question in feminism.* Ithaca, NY: Cornell University Press.

Harley, S. (1990). For the good of family and race: Gender, work and domestic roles in the black community, 1880–1930. In M. R. Malson, E. Mudimbe-Boyi, J. F. O'Barr, & M. Wyer (Eds.), *Black women in America: Social science perspectives* (pp. 159–172). Chicago: University of Chicago Press.

Harragan, B. (1981). *Games mother never taught you.* New York: Warner.

Harrison, B. W. (1985). *Making the connections: Essays in feminist social ethics* (C. S. Robb, Ed.). Boston: Beacon.

Haslinger, S. (1996). Objective reality, male reality, and social construction. In A. Garry & M. Pearsall (Eds.), *Women, knowledge, and reality: Explorations in feminist philosophy* (pp. 84–107). New York and London: Routledge.

Hearn, J., & Parkin, P. W. (1988). Women, men, and leadership: A critical review of assumptions, practice and change in the industrialized nations. In N. J. Adler & D. N. Israeli (Eds.), *Women in management worldwide* (pp. 17–40). Armonk, NY: Sharpe.

Helgesen, S. (1990). *The female advantage: Women's ways of leadership.* New York: Doubleday.

Heller, T. (1982). *Women and men as leaders: In business, educational and social service organizations.* New York: Praeger.

Hendricks, J. J. (1992). Women-centered reality and rational legalism. *Administration & Society, 23*(4), 455–470.

Hickman, C. (1990). *Mind of a manager, soul of a leader.* New York: John Wiley.

Hochschild, A. (1989). *The second shift: Working parents and the revolution at home.* New York: Viking.

Hoffman, J. (1999, June 30). How Rocky Jones got her fire captain's bars, after years of smoke and mirrors. *New York Times,* p. A22.

Hofstadter, R. (1963). *Anti-intellectualism in American life.* New York: Knopf.

Holden, M. (1996). *Continuity and disruption: Essays in public administration.* Pittsburgh: University of Pittsburgh Press.

Honig, B. (1993). *Political theory and the displacement of politics.* Ithaca, NY: Cornell University Press.

Holusha, J. (1991, May 5). Grace Pastiak's "web of inclusion." *New York Times,* Sec. 3, pp. 1, 6.

Hudson Institute. (1988). *Civil service 2000.* Washington, DC: Government Printing Office.

Immediate work. (1912). *The Survey, 29*(7), 189.

"Iron Lady" attacks sexual political double standard. (1990, September 14). *The Olympian,* p. A1.

Jacques, R. (1996). *Manufacturing the employee: Management knowledge from the 19th to the 21st centuries.* London: Sage.

Jaggar, A. (1983). *Feminist politics and human nature.* Totowa, NJ: Rowman & Allenheld.

Jamison, K. H. (1995). *Beyond the double bind: Women and leadership.* New York and Oxford: Oxford University Press.

Johnson, B. (1987). *A world of difference.* Baltimore: Johns Hopkins University Press.

Johnson, T. H. (1960). *The complete poems of Emily Dickinson.* Boston: Little, Brown.

Kanter, R. M. (1977). *Men and women of the corporation.* New York: Basic Books.

Kanter, R. M. (1980). Women and the structure of organizations: Explorations in theory and behavior. In C. W. Konek, S. L. Kitch, & G. E. Hammond (Eds.), *Design for equity: Women and leadership in higher education* (pp. 49–63). Newton, MA: Educational Development Center.

Kass, H. D. (1990). Stewardship as a fundamental element in images of public administration. In H. D. Kass & B. L. Catron (Eds.), *Images and identities in public administration* (pp. 113–131). Newbury Park, CA: Sage.

Kearny, R. C., & Sinha, C. (1988). Professionalism and bureaucratic responsiveness: Conflict or compatibility. *Public Administration Review, 48*(1), 571–579.

Keller, E. F. (1985). *Reflections on gender and science.* New Haven, CT: Yale University Press.

Keller, E. F., & Grontkowski, C. (1983). The mind's eye. In S. Harding & M. B. Hintikka (Eds.), *Discovering reality* (pp. 207–224). Dordrecht, The Netherlands: Reidel.

Keller, L. F. (1988). A heritage from Rome: The administrator as doer. *Dialogue: The Public Administration Theory Network, 10*(2), 49–75.

Kelley, R. E. (1989). In praise of followers. In W. E. Rosenbach & R. L. Taylor (Eds.), *Contemporary issues in leadership* (2nd ed., pp. 124–134). Boulder, CO: Westview.

Kerber, L. K. (1980). *Women of the republic: Intellect and ideology in revolutionary America.* New York: Norton.

Kerfoot, D., & Knights, D. (1996). "The best is yet to come?": The quest for embodiment in managerial work. In D. L. Collinson & J. Hearn (Eds.), *Men as managers, managers as men: Critical perspectives on men, masculinities and managements* (pp. 78–98). London: Sage.

Kets de Vries, M. F. R. (1989). *Prisons of leadership.* New York: John Wiley.

Kilborn, P. T. (1995, March 16). Women and minorities still face "glass ceiling." *New York Times,* p. C22.

King, C. S. (1992). *Gender and management: Men, women and decision making in public organizations.* Unpublished doctoral dissertation, University of Colorado, Denver.

King, C. S., Stivers, C., & Collaborators. (1998). *Government is us: Public administration in an anti-government era.* Thousand Oaks, CA: Sage.

Kotter, J. P. (1990, May-June). What leaders really do. *Harvard Business Review,* pp. 103–111.

Kraditor, A. (1968). *Up from the pedestal: Selected writing in the history of American feminism.* Chicago: Quadrangle Books.

Krislov, S. (1974). *Representative bureaucracy.* Englewood Cliffs, NJ: Prentice Hall.

Landes, J. B. (1988). *Women and the public sphere in the age of the French revolution.* Ithaca, NY: Cornell University Press.

Lane, L. M., & Wolf, J. F. (1990). *The human resources crisis in the public sector: Rebuilding the capacity to govern.* Westport, CT: Quorum Books.

Lange, L. (1979). Rousseau and the general will. In L. M. G. Clark & L. Lange (Eds.), *The sexism of social and political theory: Women and reproduction from Plato to Nietzsche* (pp. 41–52). Toronto: University of Toronto Press.

Laws, J. L. (1976). Work aspirations of women: False leads and new starts. In M. Blaxall & B. Reagan (Eds.), *Women and the workplace: The implications of occupational segregation* (pp. 33–50). Chicago: University of Chicago Press.

Leach, W. (1980). *True love and perfect union: The feminist reform of sex and society.* New York: Basic Books.

Lemons, J. S. (1990). *The woman citizen: Social feminism in the 1920s.* Charlottesville: University of Virginia Press. (Original work published 1973).

Lennon, M. C., & Rosenfeld, S. (1994). Relative fairness and the division of housework: The importance of options. *American Journal of Sociology, 100*(2), 506–531.

Lerner, G. (1979). *The majority finds its past: Placing women in history.* New York: Oxford University Press.

Lerner, G. (1986). *The creation of patriarchy.* New York: Oxford University Press.

Lewin, T. (1994, October 15). Working women say bias persists. *New York Times,* p. 8.

Lewis, E. (1980). *Public entrepreneurship: Toward a theory of bureaucratic political power.* Bloomington: Indiana University Press.

Long, N. E. (1981). The S.E.S. and the public interest. *Public Administration Review, 41*(3), 305–311.

Lubove, R. (1965). *Professional altruism: The emergence of social work as a career, 1880–1930.* Cambridge, MA: Harvard University Press.

Lynn, L. E., Jr. (1996). *Public management as art, science and profession.* Chatham, NJ: Chatham House.

Maccoby, M. (1988). *Why work? Motivating and leading the new generation.* New York: Simon & Schuster.

Mainzer, L. C. (1964, January). Honor in bureaucratic life. *Review of Politics, 26,* 70–90.

Major, B. (1993). Gender, entitlement, and the distribution of family labor. *Journal of Social Issues, 49*(3), 141–159.

Manning, M. (1989). *Leadership skills for women: Achieving impact as a manager* (with P. Haddock). Los Altos, CA: Crisp.

Markus, M. (1987). Women, success and civil society: Submission to, or subversion of, the achievement principle. In S. Benhabib & D. Cornell (Eds.), *Feminism as critique* (pp. 96–109). Minneapolis: University of Minnesota Press.

McSwite, O. C. (1997). *Legitimacy in public administration: A discourse analysis*. Thousand Oaks, CA: Sage.

Merchant, C. (1980). *The death of nature: Women, ecology, and the scientific revolution*. San Francisco: Harper & Row.

Milbank, D. (2001, January 8–14). The Vice President as prime minister. *Washington Post Weekly*, pp. 6–9.

Miller, W., Kerr, B., & Reid, M. (1999). A national study of gender-based occupational segregation in municipal bureaucracies: Persistence of glass walls? *Public Administration Review, 59*(3), 218–230.

Milwid, B. (1990). *Working with men: Professional women talk about power, sexuality, and ethics*. Hillsboro, OR: Beyond Words Publishing.

Mintzberg, H. (1973). *The nature of managerial work*. New York: Harper & Row.

Mitchell, T. (1991). The limits of the state: Beyond statist approaches and their critics. *American Political Science Review, 85*(1), 79–96.

Mitchell, T. R., & Scott, W. G. (1987). Leadership failures, the distrusting public, and prospects of the administrative state. *Public Administration Review, 47*(6), 445–452.

Moi, T. (1985). *Sexual/textual politics: Feminist literary theory*. London: Routledge.

Morgan, D. F. (1990). Administrative *phronesis*: Discretion and the problem of administrative legitimacy in our constitutional system. In H. D. Kass & B. L. Catron (Eds.), *Images and identities in public administration* (pp. 67–86). Newbury Park, CA: Sage.

Morgan, D. F., & Kass, H. D. (1991). Constitutional stewardship, *phronesis*, and the American administrative ethos. *Dialogue: The Public Administration Theory Network, 12*(1), 17–60.

Morton, N. O., & Lindquist, S. A. (1997). Revealing the feminist in Mary Parker Follett. *Administration & Society, 29*(3), 348–371.

Mosher, F. C. (1968). *Democracy and the public service*. New York: Oxford University Press.

Muncy, R. (1991). *Creating a female dominion in American reform, 1890–1935*. New York: Oxford University Press.

Nalbandian, J. (1990). Tenets of contemporary professionalism in local government. *Public Administration Review, 50*(6), 654–662.

Neverdon-Morton, C. (1989). *Afro-American women of the South and the advancement of the race, 1895–1925*. Knoxville: University of Tennessee Press.

Noble, B. P. (1993, August 15). The debate over la différence. *New York Times Current Events Edition*, p. 36.

Noble, D. F. (1992). *A world without women: The Christian clerical culture of Western science*. New York and Oxford: Oxford University Press.

Oates, S. B. (1994). *A woman of valor: Clara Barton and the Civil War*. New York: Macmillan.

O'Brien, M. (1989). *Reproducing the world: Essays in feminist theory*. Boulder, CO: Westview.

Okin, S. M. (1979). *Women in Western political thought*. Princeton, NJ: Princeton University Press.

Okin, S. M. (1989). *Justice, gender and the family*. New York: Basic Books.

O'Leary, R., & Wise, C. R. (1991). Public managers, judges, and legislators: Redefining the new partnership. *Public Administration Review, 51*(4), 316–327.

Osborne, D., & Gaebler, T. (1992). *Reinventing government: How the entrepreneurial spirit is transforming the public sector*. New York: Penguin Books.

Pateman, C. (1989). *The disorder of women: Democracy, feminism, and political theory*. Stanford, CA: Stanford University Press.

Patterson, P. (2001). Introduction [to Symposium—Reinventing the public body]. *Administrative Theory & Praxis, 23*(2), 175–186.

Person, H. (1926). Basic principles of administration and of management: Scientific management. In H. C. Metcalf (Ed.), *Scientific foundations of business administration* (pp. 204–217). Baltimore: Williams and Wilkins.

Peterson, I. (1992, February 2). These data, the enumerator always wrings twice. *New York Times*, p. E3.

Pitkin, H. F. (1984). *Fortune is a woman: Gender and politics in the thought of Niccolo Machiavelli*. Berkeley: University of California Press.

Poggi, G. (1978). *The development of the modern state: A sociological introduction*. Stanford, CA: Stanford University Press.

Poggi, G. (1990). *The state: Its nature, development and prospects*. Stanford, CA: Stanford University Press.

Potts, M., & Behr, P. (1987). *The leading edge: CEOs who turned their companies around: What they did and how they did it*. New York: McGraw-Hill.

Powell, G. N. (1993). *Women and men in management* (2nd ed.). Newbury Park, CA: Sage.

Powell, G. N. (1999). Reflections on the glass ceiling: Recent trends and future prospects. In G. N. Powell (Ed.), *Handbook of gender and organizations* (pp. 325–345). Thousand Oaks, CA: Sage.

Pringle, R. (1989). Bureaucracy, rationality, and sexuality: The case of secretaries. In J. Hearn, D. L. Sheppard, P. Tancred-Sheriff, & G. Burrell (Eds.), *The sexuality of organization* (pp. 158–177). London: Sage.

Pugh, D. L. (1989). Professionalism in public administration: Problems, perspectives and the role of ASPA. *Public Administration Review, 49*(1), 1–8.

Rhode, D. (1988). Perspectives on professional women. *Stanford Law Review, 40*, 1163–1207.

Richardson, W. D., & Adkins, S. R. (1997). Understanding ethics through literature: Character, honor, and the corruption of body and soul in King Rat. *Administration & Society, 29*(2), 201–221.

Roberts, S. (1995, April 27). Women's work: What's new, what isn't. *New York Times*, p. A12.

Rohr, J. A. (1986). *To run a constitution: The legitimacy of the American administrative state.* Lawrence: University Press of Kansas.

Rohr, J. A. (1989). Public administration, executive power and constitutional confusion. *Public Administration Review, 49*(2), 108–114.

Roos, P. A., & Gatta, M. L. (1999). The gender gap in earnings: Trends, explanations, and prospects. In G. N. Powell (Ed.), *Handbook of gender and work* (pp. 95–123). Thousand Oaks, CA: Sage.

Rosenbloom, D. H. (1987). Public administration and the judiciary: The "new partnership." *Public Administration Review, 49*(2), 108–114.

Rosener, J. B. (1990, November-December). Ways women lead. *Harvard Business Review,* pp. 119–125.

Rossi, A. S. (Ed.). (1973). *The feminist papers: From Adams to de Beauvoir.* New York: Columbia University Press.

Rourke, F. E. (1992). Responsiveness and neutral competence in American bureaucracy. *Public Administration Review, 52*(6), 539–546.

Ruddick, S. (1989). *Maternal thinking: Toward a politics of peace.* Boston: Beacon.

Saxonhouse, A. (1985). *Women in the history of political thought.* New York: Praeger.

Schreurs, P. (2000). *Enchanting rationality: An analysis of rationality in the Anglo-American discourse on public organization.* Delft, The Netherlands: Uitgeverij Eburon.

Scott, J. W. (1989). Gender: a useful category of historical analysis. In E. Weed (Ed.), *Coming to terms: Feminism, theory, politics* (pp. 81–100). New York: Routledge.

Selznick, P. (1957). *Leadership in administration: A sociological interpretation.* Evanston, IL: Row, Peterson.

Settlement pioneers in city government. (1914, February 21). *Charities and the Commons,* pp. 638–639.

Sheppard, D. L. (1989). Organizations, power and sexuality: The image and self-image of women managers. In J. Hearn, D. L. Sheppard, P. Tancred-Sheriff, & G. Burrell (Eds.), *The sexuality of organization* (pp. 139–157). London: Sage.

Sherman, N. (1989). *The fabric of character: Aristotle's theory of virtue.* Oxford, UK: Clarendon.

Sherwood, F. (1997). Responding to the decline in public service professionalism. *Public Administration Review, 59*(3), 21–27.

Shklar, J. N. (1991). *American citizenship: The quest for inclusion.* London: Harvard University Press.

Simkhovitch, M. K. (1906, September 1). Settlement organization. *Charities and the Commons*, pp. 566–569.

Simkhovitch, M. K. (1938). *Neighborhood: My story of Greenwich House.* New York: Norton.

Skowronek, S. (1982). *Building a new American state: The expansion of national administrative capacities, 1877–1920.* Cambridge, UK: Cambridge University Press.

Sterling, D. (Ed.). (1984). *We are your sisters: Black women in the nineteenth century.* New York: Norton.

Stever, J. A. (1988). *The end of public administration: Problems of the profession in the post-Progressive era.* Dobbs Ferry, NY: Transnational.

Stivers, C. (1990a). Active citizenship and public administration. In G. Wamsley, R. Bacher, C. Goodsell, P. Kronenberg, J. Rohr, C. Stivers, O. White, & J. Wolf, *Refounding public administration* (pp. 246–273). Newbury Park, CA: Sage.

Stivers, C. (1990b). Toward a feminist theory of public administration. *Women and Politics, 10*(4), 49–65.

Stivers, C. (1991). Why can't a woman be less like a man? Women's leadership dilemma. *Journal of Nursing Administration, 21*(5), 47–51.

Stivers, C. (1992a). Beverlee A. Myers: Power, virtue and womanhood in public administration. In T. L. Cooper & N. D. Wright (Eds.), *Exemplary public administrators: Character and leadership in government* (pp. 166–172). San Francisco: Jossey-Bass.

Stivers, C. (1992b). A wild patience: A feminist critique of ameliorative public administration. In M. T. Bailey & R. T. Mayer (Eds.), *Public management in an interconnected world: Essays in the Minnowbrook tradition* (pp. 53–74). Westport, CT: Greenwood.

Stivers, C. (1994). The listening bureaucrat: Responsiveness in public administration. *Public Administration Review, 53*(4), 364–369.

Stivers, C. (1996a). Mary Parker Follett and the question of gender. *Organization, 3*(1), 161–166.

Stivers, C. (1996b). Refusing to get it right: Citizenship, difference, and the Refounding project. In G. Wamsley & J. Wolf (Eds.), *Refounding democratic public administration* (pp. 260–278). Thousand Oaks, CA: Sage.

Stivers, C. (2000a). *Bureau men, settlement women: Constructing public administration in the Progressive era.* Lawrence: University Press of Kansas.

Stivers, C. (2000b). Citizenship ethics in public administration. In T. L. Cooper (Ed.), *Handbook of administrative ethics* (2nd ed., pp. 435–456). New York: Marcel Dekker.

Stroh, L. K., Brett, J. M., & Reilly, A. H. (1992). All the right stuff: A comparison of female and male managers' career progression. *Journal of Applied Psychology, 77*(3), 251–160.

Stroh, L. K., & Reilly, A. H. (1999). Gender and careers: Present experiences and emerging trends. In G. N. Powell (Ed.), *Handbook of gender and work* (pp. 307–324). Thousand Oaks, CA: Sage.

Taylor, F. W. (1911). *The principles of scientific management.* New York: Harper.

Terry, L. D. (1990). Leadership in the administrative state: The concept of administrative conservatorship. *Administration and Society, 21*(4), 395–412.

Terry, L. D. (1991). The public administrator as hero: All that glitters is not gold: Rejoinder to Christopher Bellavita's "The public administrator as hero." *Administration & Society, 23*(2), 186–193.

Thompson, K. W. (1985). *The credibility of institutions, policies and leadership, Vol. 18: Essays on leadership. Comparative insights.* Lanham, MD: University Press of America.

Tichy, N., & Ulrich, D. (1984). Revitalizing organizations: The leadership role. In J. R. Kimberly & R. E. Quinn (Eds.), *New futures: The challenge of managing corporate transitions* (pp. 240–265). Homewood, IL: Dow Jones Irwin.

Trained social workers take charge of New York City government. (1914, January 10). *The Survey,* pp. 430–433.

Travis, D. J. (1991). *Racism American style: A corporate gift.* Chicago: Urban Research Press.

U.S. Bureau of the Census. (1940). *Statistical abstract of the United States.* Washington, DC: Government Printing Office.

U.S. Bureau of the Census. (1960). *Statistical abstract of the United States.* Washington, DC: Government Printing Office.

U.S. Bureau of the Census. (1990). *Statistical abstract of the United States.* Washington, DC: Government Printing Office.

U.S. Bureau of the Census. (1999). *Statistical abstract of the United States.* Washington, DC: Government Printing Office.

U.S. Glass Ceiling Commission. (1995). *Good for business: Making full use of the nation's human capital.* Washington, DC: Government Printing Office.

U.S. Office of Personnel Management. (1998). *Central personnel data file* (CPDF). Available: http://www.opm.gov/feddata/demograp/1998

U.S. Office of Personnel Management. (2000). *Central personnel data file* (CPDF). Available: http://www.opm.gov/feddata/demograp.htm

Valian, V. (1998). *Why so slow? The advancement of women.* Cambridge, MA and London: MIT Press.

Van Riper, P. P. (1983). The American administrative state: Wilson and the founders—an unorthodox view. *Public Administration Review, 43*(6), 477–490.

Vollmer, H. M., & Mills, D. L. (Eds.). (1966). *Professionalization.* Englewood Cliffs, NJ: Prentice Hall.

Wajcman, J. (1996). Desperately seeking differences: Is management style gendered? *British Journal of Industrial Relations, 34*(3), 333–349.

Waldo, D. (1948). *The administrative state.* New York: Ronald Press.

Wamsley, G. L. (1990). The agency perspective: Public administrators as agential leaders. In G. L. Wamsley, R. N. Bacher, C. T. Goodsell, P. S. Kronenberg, J. A. Rohr, C. M. Stivers, O. F. White, & J. A. Wolf, *Refounding public administration* (pp. 114–162). Newbury Park, CA: Sage.

Wamsley, G. L., Bacher, R. N., Goodsell, C. T., Kronenberg, P. S., Rohr, J. A., Stivers, C. M., White, O. F., & Wolf, J. F. (1990). *Refounding public administration.* Newbury Park, CA: Sage.

Warner, M. (1981). *Joan of Arc: The image of female heroism.* New York: Knopf.

Wells, T. (1973, Summer). The covert power of gender in organizations. *Journal of Contemporary Business,* pp. 53–68.

Welter, B. (1976). The cult of true womanhood, 1820–1860. In B. Welter, *Dimity convictions: The American woman in the 19th century* (pp. 21–41). Athens: Ohio University Press.

White, L. D. (1948). *The federalists.* New York: Macmillan.

White, L. D. (1951). The *Jeffersonians.* New York: Macmillan.

Wiebe, R. H. (1967). *The search for order, 1877–1920.* New York: Hill & Wang.

Wildavsky, A. (1990). Administration with hierarchy? Bureaucracy without authority? In N. B. Lynn & A. Wildavsky (Eds.), *Public administration: The state of the discipline* (pp. xiii-xix). Chatham, NJ: Chatham House.

Wills, G. (1984). *Cincinnatus: George Washington and the enlightenment.* Garden City, NY: Doubleday.

Wilson, J. Q. (1989). *Bureaucracy: What government agencies do and why they do it.* New York: Basic Books.

Wilson, W. (1887). The study of administration. *Political Science Quarterly, 2*(2), 197–222.

Woods, R. A. (1906, January 16). Social work: A new profession. *Charities and the Commons, 15,* pp. 469–476.

Woods, R. A., & Kennedy, A. J. (1970). *The settlement horizon: A national estimate.* New York: Arno Press. (Original work published 1922).

Wyzomirski, M. J. (1987). The politics of art: Nancy Hanks and the National Endowment for the Arts. In J. W. Doig & E. C. Hargrove (Eds.), *Leadership and innovation: A biographical perspective on entrepreneurs in government* (pp. 207–245). Baltimore: Johns Hopkins University Press.

Young, I. M. (1987). Impartiality and the civic public. In S. Benhabib & D. Cornell (Eds.), *Feminism as critique* (pp. 57–76). Minneapolis: University of Minnesota Press.

Index